FLOWERS *for* ZION

IMMEASURABLE LOVE

LEANN WALTERS

Flowers for Zion: Immeasurable Love

Trilogy Christian Publishers A Wholly Owned Subsidary of Trinity Broadcasting Network

2442 Michelle Drive Tustin, CA 92780

Cover design by: Grant Swank

For information about special discounts for bulk purchases, please contact Trilogy Christian Publishing.

Manufactured in the United States of America

10 9 8 7 6 5 4 3 2 1

Library of Congress Cataloging-in-Publication Data is available.

ISBN: 979-8-88738-918-9

E-ISBN: 979-8-88738-919-6

Dedication

This book is dedicated to Zion—beauty for ashes...
Luke 24:45–48:

Then he opened their understanding, that they might understand the scriptures,

And said unto them, thus it is written, and thus it behooved Christ to suffer; and to rise from the dead the third day.

And that repentance and remission of sins should be preached in his name among all nations, beginning at Jerusalem.

And [you] are witnesses to these things.

Contents

Preface

This book is about the *immeasurable* love of God. God loves unconditionally—born, unborn, young, old, rebellious, or obedient. His love is not conditional or based on our behavior. It is uncontainable, freely given, and sacrificial, evidenced by His Son, Jesus, who poured out His blood on a cross, paying the ultimate sacrifice for our sins per the Scriptures. He was buried, and on the third day, Jesus rose from the dead, conquering death, hell, and the grave, according to the Scriptures. Through this act, this sacrifice is the offering of forgiveness and redemption to those who believe.

This book is about the infinite grace, mercy, and love that God extends to all through His Son, Jesus Christ, God's provision for our sin problem. My hope is that you, too, will experience this infinite, incomparable, holy, personal, *immeasurable love* by coming to know Jesus Christ as Savior and Lord. He died for you. He knows your name. He is our blessed hope!

"And now these three remain: Faith, hope, and love. But the greatest of these is Love" (1 Corinthians 13:13, NIV).

Introduction

"But none of these things move me, neither count I my life dear unto myself, so that I might finish my course with joy, and the ministry, which I have received of the Lord Jesus, to testify the Gospel of the grace of God" (Acts 20:24).

This book was written because God placed a burning fire within me to tell the stories of women and girls who found themselves in unplanned pregnancies. The purpose is for His glory. It reflects how powerful and loving He is and that His desire is that none should perish. He has paid an exceedingly high price to redeem us. The names, dates, and places have been modified so that the identity of these women and girls will remain anonymous (see the appendix for the meaning of each name given that describes her character, situation, or how God sees her). The details of their stories are true.

My motto while working at a crisis or unplanned pregnancy help center in Dallas, Texas, was, "Love is the game changer." I never liked the term "crisis" in referring to an unplanned pregnancy. Crisis best describes the thinking mode that a woman or girl goes into when she finds herself in an *unplanned* pregnancy rather than the condition of the pregnancy itself. Our best thinking is often not done in the middle of what we perceive to be a "crisis."

The definition of a crisis is:

- a time of intense difficulty or danger (catastrophe, calamity, cataclysm, emergency, disaster, plight, mess, dilemma, quandary, setback, reversal, upheaval, drama, trouble, dire straits, tough times, hardship, adversity, extremity, distress, difficulty)

- a time when a difficult or weighty decision must be made (critical point, decisive point, turning point, crossroads, critical period, crux, climax, culmination, moment of truth, zero hour, point of no return)

"Stand at the crossroads and look, ask for the ancient paths, ask what the good way is and walk in it, and you will find rest for your souls" (Jeremiah 6:16, NIV).

I never liked the "unplanned" adjective either; maybe it is unexpected for the parents, but the Bible clearly teaches that God ordains all life. He is the author and the Creator of all life, having planned each of us before the foundation of the world.

We now know that life begins at conception, and it is no longer an argument in the scientific or medical world. Today's argument in Western culture is based on when "personhood" begins. This is truly a denial of life and the rejection of truth at every level of consciousness. Truly, our nation is under judgment and is afflicted with blindness.

In eight years of pregnancy options counseling, I learned that every girl has a story. Every woman has a story. Everyone has a story. They are all unique—all known by God. Our own stories are based on a series of life events that reveal our desperate need for God in a fallen world.

Interwoven among the stories of the girls and women, babies, and men I encountered while working and volunteering at this center is my own personal story. A story that includes how, at age fifteen,

I walked into an abortion clinic in Dallas, Texas, and without the knowledge or permission of my parents, had an abortion performed before I was old enough to have a driver's license. This choice impacted the course of my life forever. Extremely far down that course of life, I encountered Jesus Christ in a radical way that forever and finally changed the journey of my life for good! There is no turning back!

Read with me and ask God to break your heart for these women and girls, to break your heart for these babies, men, and families that are forever impacted by unplanned pregnancy and, too many times, by abortion as a result. Ask God what you can do to make an impact in the culture concerning the sanctity of life. *Ask Him to show you His heart on the matter.*

There is hope! His name is Jesus! There is truth! His name is Jesus! There is a way! His name is Jesus!

There is life! His name is Jesus!

To God be the glory forever and ever, amen.

This One Runs to Me

I walked alone, a dark and unpredictable path, not one bit of it straight. The air was heavy, difficult to breathe, stifling.

The fog crept in, getting under my skin, with eerie noises behind me on the path. I pressed on.

So dark that I could not see even what was directly in front of me. The fog was blinding me; the trees were staring down at me.

A scamper and a slither off the road. Grasses were moving from the stirring.

A little slice of moonlight was peeking down through the treetops.

It was lighting my dark and winding path, and narrow with blind turns, it stretched on endlessly. I thought my heart had escaped from my chest. I thought it had fled to hide forever. Perhaps hiding in the trees amongst the branches and the leaves.

But I heard it beating loudly in my chest.

My ears were so tuned in that imperceptible sounds were amplified as if wired to loudspeakers.

The sounds were exaggerated and unnerving.

I was tired, with muscles aching. Emotionally drained. Spiritually empty.

I was fatigued to the point of lying down in the path regardless of the total darkness, minus that sliver of moonlight.

Hark to the forest animals, hark to the creepy crawly things on the forest floor, woe to the dark spirits assailing me there.

I thought to myself, *This is it; I can't do this anymore. I am done; I am undone. I can go no further. There is no end; there is no relief.*

Yet there is no sense to an ordinary life. This I cannot live. This I cannot endure. I would prefer you to take me now!

This path is too hard; it is dark, scary, and unpredictable.

But an ordinary life is no life at all! I cannot live it; You made me. You know this. Allow me to bask in Your presence in light and peace; resurrect my heart to a new life! There is no air left here to breathe. "Father, Jesus, help me!"

Suddenly a mighty wind!

The grasses bent, and the branches of the trees began to sway.

A piercing, blinding light beamed from the sky.

The path became illuminated with the purest of light.

The fog lifted and dissipated.

The twists and turns were smoothing out before my eyes. A minute earlier I was sure I would die.

The air became crisp and clean and light and easy. The forest animals and creepy crawly things subdued.

The dark spirits that claimed that path as their territory disappeared.

My hair blew up from the back of my neck, the mighty wind tossing it about.

The sound of the roaring water just below! Unbeknownst to me until this moment, I had been walking alongside the edge of a cliff, the ocean playing below.

Waves crashing into the beach, a life of their own, roaring onto the sand in a symphonic melody of uniqueness each and every one.

Why doubt? Why despair?

"Come with Me, My child, and see." I took His hand.

A picture of heaven! I saw Jesus sitting on a tree trunk in a white linen robe. He was speaking to someone whose face was obscure. But whose presence was known.

I saw Him up ahead, and I ran to Him at full speed.

He turned and stood just in time for me to jump in His arms. I grabbed Him and hugged Him, and I wouldn't let go.

He turned back to the one to whom He was speaking and said:

"This one runs to Me."

My life will never be ordinary; I am a wave in a symphonic melody pouring out of the ocean of love and onto this temporary shore of life. Unique. Known.

He is my beloved, and I am His.

He whispered in my ear, "This one runs to Me."

Beulah: Clothed in Robes of Righteousness

Beulah came into the center with a friend, an older lady with a well-worn face and an air of authority. Beulah had a fresh young face with bright brown eyes framed by sandy blonde hair. She had a sprinkling of freckles across her nose and on her cheeks, which made her look even younger than her thirty-two years. She had a pretty smile that lit up her countenance when it broke free from her lips. Beulah needed a pregnancy test, and her boyfriend's mother (we'll call her Grace) had driven her to the center.

Beulah was from Oklahoma, now living in Dallas with her boyfriend and Grace. She had difficulty filling out her paperwork, and I realized that she had a challenging time reading and writing. Her signature reflected the handwriting of a preteen. Her spelling was lacking, and she did not complete a large part of the intake sheet. Several answers on the form were inappropriate, and it was clear the questions were not understood.

"Beulah, did you understand all the questions? It looks like you left many of the questions blank," I commented as I scanned her intake form.

She looked at me and smiled that beautiful smile of hers and said, "No. I'm dumb. I mean, I'm not stupid, but I'm not smart. I'm disabled, and I have papers from the state of Oklahoma saying that I am dumb and I am disabled."

"Oh," I replied. "Do you have difficulty reading and writing?"

"Yes," she replied. "I can't work because I can't read and write, and that's why my boyfriend's momma brought me here today."

"It's okay," I said. "We'll go through these forms together." I went through all the intake forms with her and completed them with her answers to all the questions.

Beulah had met her boyfriend at a truck stop. "He's cute, and he's not fat," she revealed. "And he is really sweet, not like most truck drivers," she said as she conspiratorially winked her eye at me, making a face like I understood what she was implying. She explained that she had spent a week with him at his motel, and they had enjoyed swimming and spending time together while he was between trips. Beulah explained that her sister had even joined her at the motel to hang out with her and her new friend and enjoy the pool for about a week.

I mentally noted that Beulah had a large dragon tattoo on her chest and a matching smaller one on her foot that wound around her ankle. I was thinking about this tattoo, the story of how she met her boyfriend, and the ensuing relationship that now brought her into our pregnancy center seeking a pregnancy test. Beulah explained to me that she had three other children who were temporarily living with her mother until she could get into a more stable situation that would allow her to regain custody.

It was clear that Beulah loved her children. She was excited about the prospect of another pregnancy and having a child with her new boyfriend. Beulah explained she was living with him and Grace until they could get on their feet and get their own place. Grace was truly kind to Beulah and displayed support for the relationship with her son and the resulting pregnancy.

I shared the Gospel with Beulah, and she shared with me that she knew Jesus and that He was her Lord and Savior. She explained that a social service agency in Oklahoma had taught her about God's love and how she had accepted Christ as Lord of her life. Her face beamed as she spoke about how God's love had gotten her through tough times—including past abusive relationships, losing custody of her children (due to her problematic employment situation), and her "disability." She made it noticeably clear she intended to get all her children back.

Beulah's test was positive. She was ecstatic. She wanted to join our parenting classes, a "learn while you earn" program. I prayed with Beulah about her pregnancy and her future, including her health, her relationship with her boyfriend, and her relationship with Christ. We talked about God's plan for the family, marriage, and children. Beulah shared that she hoped to marry soon and ultimately regain custody of all her children.

We helped Beulah plan the commute to our center so she could return to the classes she signed up for. She was unable to drive since she could not read and, therefore, was unable to get a driver's license. With help, she could manage the light rail system and commute to our center to participate in parenting classes.

After I left the center that Saturday, Beulah was in my heart and mind, and I could not stop thinking of her. She seemed so innocent in a way; her mannerisms were childlike, and her communication straightforward. There was no shame in her disability and no self-pity implied in any of her stories.

Every girl who came into our center had a story. Every story was unique. Every story was important. Every appointment was a divine one. That Saturday afternoon, after I left the center and Beulah was in my thoughts, God impressed upon me that Beulah was a prostitute. It all made sense. She could not get a normal job with her disability. My impression was that her boyfriend was likely once a "client" from the truck stop she worked. My heart broke for her, and I cried thinking about her predicament. How could she make a living? How could she support her children? This man seemed to have extended kindness and, ultimately, real affection to her. Beulah shared with me that he told her he loved her smile and that she made him laugh. He wanted her to keep their baby and brought her to Dallas to get away from the "life" she had in Oklahoma.

He had brought her home to his momma, and she had received Beulah and tried to help her. Grace had even accompanied her to our center. She was anxious to hear if she was going to be a grandmother and prepared to help in any way she could. I had observed how kind she was toward Beulah in the waiting room. I thought about how Beulah's face lit up when she spoke about Jesus. I knew her relationship with Him was real. I thought to myself, *But, Lord, she is (or was) a prostitute. How can this be?*

The Lord spoke to me in my spirit and said, "Because she is clothed in robes of righteousness. When I look at Beulah, I see her clothed in the righteousness of My Son, Jesus. She is covered with the righteousness of Christ."

Isaiah 61:10 (NKJV):

"I will greatly rejoice in the LORD, my soul shall be joyful in my God; for he has clothed me with the garments of salvation, he has covered me with the robe of righteousness, as a bridegroom decks himself with ornaments, and as a bride adorns herself with her jewels."

My heart was filled with love for Beulah. I loved her. When I thought of her, I pictured her clothed in a beautiful, long, purple royal robe. I saw her through the eyes of Jesus, and she was beautiful, radiant. Her face shone with the radiance of Christ.

Beulah's story is the first in this book because her story *is the Gospel.* The Gospel of Christ is to believe and be saved, simple enough for a child to understand. Jesus told the thief on the cross as they were both dying that he "would be in paradise" with Him that day. This blows away any "works-based" *salvation* requirement.

When a crowd asked Jesus, *"What shall we do, that we might work the works of God?"* (John 6:28), Jesus replied in John 6:29:

"This is the work of God, that [you] believe in him whom he [has] sent."

In verse forty of John, Jesus said:

"And this is the will of him that sent me, that everyone which [sees] the Son, and [believes] in him, may have everlasting life: and I will raise him up at the last day."

Ephesians 2:8–9 reads:

"For by grace are [you] saved through faith: and that not of yourselves; it is the gift of God: Not of works, lest any man should boast."

"I will sing unto the Lord as long as I live: I will sing praise to my God while I have my being. My meditation of him shall be sweet: I will be glad in the Lord."

Psalm 104:33–34

Reduction

(Creation of a Savory Sauce)

I must become less so that He can become more. Lord, help me to be like You.

Help my life reflect Your selflessness.

If I never hear another word of affirmation from humanity, let Your love be enough.

Let Your sweet voice whispering in my ear, "You are loved," totally captivate my being.

Bring that moment to the forefront of my memory so that I might recollect the sweetness of it. Greater than the intimate whisper of a lover.

Oh, You, Great and Glorious One, the lover of my soul. Everyone knows that reduction produces the most flavor. *Lord, my prayer is this: conform me to Your image.*

Abandoned

It was Memorial Day weekend, and my mother, sister, and I were at my grandparents' house in Olney, Texas. My grandparents lived on a farm west of town. My grandfather was a cotton farmer, and my grandparents lived on almost ninety acres that included a stock pond and a garden full of watermelons and cantaloupe. My grandmother's kitchen always smelled good, with a typical daily menu consisting of homemade biscuits with gravy and bacon for breakfast, fried chicken and mashed potatoes, or hamburgers grilled outside with baked beans on the side for dinner.

My papa always greeted us at the door when we arrived, scooping us up into his arms and making a big production upon our arrival. He always had a pack of Juicy Fruit gum in his shirt pocket and offered it to us before we could get in the door. We never turned it down! My "mamma" always had something sweet baked, usually a great southern style "pound cake." She always had the cake in a glass pedestal cake dish with a glass lid that proudly displayed the contents. If the cake had been sliced prior to our arrival, a piece of white bread would be placed up against the "sliced" end to ensure it remained moist.

Papa would make us Coke floats when we visited. He served them to us in glass pedestal glasses that had a huge round bowl-like top that ensured plenty of space for lots of ice cream and Coke. This was a huge treat for us, and we looked forward to it each time we went for a visit.

The smell of my grandparents' house was always a comfort and joy to me as a child. I loved to indulge in all the tasty food and treats there. I enjoyed the feeling of love that pervaded my grandparent's home. It was a simple time when simple pleasures, such as skipping rocks in my grandfather's pond and picking tomatoes, watermelons, and cantaloupe from his garden, were satisfying and comforting.

My grandfather loved to tell a story of when I was a little girl and my grandparents still lived in town (before they moved to the farm) and I rode with him in his Dodge pick-up one morning to go feed the cows. We drove up in the field with a load of hay and feed, and the cows would come running when they heard the sound of my papa's truck. We fed them and put out "salt licks" for them to lick on. This was, in some way I could not comprehend at the time, beneficial to them. The fields were full of prickly pear cacti. One morning when I accompanied him, I needed to go to the toilet, and he tried to get me to go in the field behind a tree. No way would I relieve myself in the great outdoors accompanied by prickly pears! I insisted he take me back to town to use the toilet, convinced the needles would jump off of them and into my backside! He drove me back to town and gave me a tough time all the way back about being a "city slicker." He laughed hysterically at the thought that this "city" girl had to be driven all the way back to town to relieve herself due to prickly pears in the field, and he told everyone he knew the story.

My younger brother did not come with us for the long weekend on this Memorial Day trip. I cannot remember exactly why, but he stayed behind with my father for the weekend. It was halfway through the weekend when the phone rang at my grandparents' house, and it was for my mother. It was my uncle Brian, my dad's brother. It was highly unusual for him to call at my maternal grandparent's home. My mother was very distraught and upset about what was being said on the other end of the phone line. We were all being incredibly quiet, listening closely, as we knew something was terribly wrong.

My mother hung up the phone and said, "Buck is missing." My father's name was Henry Gary, but everyone called him "Buck" or "Bucky." My mother said we had to go home to help find him. He had gone to work on Saturday morning and never returned home. My anxious twelve-year-old brother had waited until dark and then ridden across town on his bike to my uncle Brian's house to seek help. My brother was left alone and confused; we were all terrified, as disappearance was known to have disastrous implications for my family.

My father had visited my school exactly once in my entire educational career. I was in the second grade in Ms. Harris' classroom at Bullock Elementary in Garland, Texas. Miss Harris was a beautiful tall, thin, bleached blonde with horn-rimmed glasses. She wore sheath dresses every day with fashionable pumps. It was the late 1960s, and Miss Harris always sported the latest fashions. She was very trendy in a classy schoolteacher kind of way. I adored her. In addition to her impeccable fashion, Miss Harris was extremely sweet. I was her pet. She often asked me to do special chores for her, such as handing out papers or passing out pencils. I often was the first in my class to finish my work, and she would look for projects for me to keep me busy.

I loved going to school and sitting in her classroom. Miss Harris cared for each of the children in that room. She was very loving, caring, and engaging. Being in her classroom gave me a feeling of warmth and security. This temporary respite was all shattered the day my father appeared at my classroom door in a suit. I immediately knew something was wrong because my father never wore a suit. He was a home appliance repairman, and he went to work in uniforms with his name stitched on the shirt pocket. He never came to my school. The fact that he was now standing in the doorway of Miss Harris' classroom was alarming.

I sat in my chair and just stared at him until Miss Harris called and waved me over to the door. She explained to me that I was leaving early with my father that day and that he would explain to me more after we left. She gave me a big hug after I gathered my things to leave. I turned to leave and walked through the classroom door and down the hall with my father. He never said a word until we got into the car. I kept wondering silently as to the whereabouts of my mother. I often walked to and from school each day. If anyone dropped me off or picked me up, it was my mother. I knew something was terribly wrong; my father's face was set in stone and silent. His jaw was tight, and he stared straight ahead.

Finally, he said, "Your uncle Oscar went missing for three days. They found him dead today on the side of the road. He was on his way to the bank to make a deposit, and they found his body in his car on the side of the road. The money was missing, and he had been shot in the head."

Stunned, my seven-year-old brain simply could not process this information. I did not know what to say. I was not close to my uncle

Oscar, and in fact, I barely knew him. We sat in complete silence on the short ride home.

Missing person reports did not seem to end well. To simply disappear without a word, without a trace, was a sure sign of something very wrong, something very sinister, as I knew from my past. My mother was obviously upset. I was fourteen years old, and my thoughts immediately went back to the last missing person experience I had in the second grade. I believed my father to be dead. I fully expected to return home to Garland, Texas, and someone would meet us at the door of our house and tell us that my father was dead and that his body had been found on the side of the road.

It was a long journey home that Memorial Day weekend, from the excitement, warmth, joy, and the loving embrace of my grandparents to the dreadful unknown. In my mind, there was sure to be a dark and sinister end to my father's mysterious disappearance. When we arrived home, my brother was quiet, clearly shaken. My mother showed extraordinarily little emotion.

My father had gone missing all right. However, he had not been attacked, robbed, or killed like my uncle seven years earlier. His car was not found on the side of the road with his dead body inside. My father was at his mistress's home. He had taken quite the sabbatical from his twelve-year-old son, his wife, and his family that long holiday weekend.

To this day I will never understand why my father chose to abandon our family in this way. Why he did not simply tell my mother that he was leaving her is beyond even my adult comprehension.

Why he would bring a tender twelve-year-old boy into this by leaving him completely alone with no explanation defies any sort of reason or logic. He had demonstrated complete abandonment to all of us, but he had made it personal to my brother that day.

Love Starvation

Our culture suffers from love starvation. The world suffers from it.

Not the world's cheap love that is perverted and offered with strings attached—quid pro quo.

"Love" has been reduced to commerce, a transaction of exchange to selfishly give to someone who is needy in order to selfishly take what one desires.

Humanity starves for pure love that is unconditional, unselfish, with no expectation of a payback.

So many vices are a result of a love-starved, depraved soul. Human beings in search of human love.

Longing for significance, uniqueness, affirmation. Longing to be nurtured.

Longing to be touched affectionately in love that asks for nothing in return. Desiring to be valued.

Desiring to be treasured.

Seeking fulfillment for the void of love in life in a variety of desperate moves.

Searching for a pure love that cannot be found in worldly love. Longing to share life with another human being who genuinely cares, who will engage that desperate soul.

Longing to be loved unconditionally. The world is starving for love.

If we understood how much God genuinely loves us, it would change the world.

We would stop looking for human love to fill that God-sized void in our heart that only He can fill.

It's always about love. Love is the game changer. Love is our testimony.

Chloe: Looks Are Deceiving

Chloe walked into our center one evening looking very fresh and professional. I almost mistook her for a salesperson or a vendor coming to visit our center rather than a client with an appointment. Chloe's whole countenance was one of great seriousness.

She was dressed in business attire, mid-twenties, and was an exceptionally beautiful young woman. She completed her paperwork efficiently and promptly and was ready to be taken back for counseling. She came to the center unaccompanied. She presented herself as poised and confident.

As I reviewed her intake forms, which included things like sexual and pregnancy history, I noticed something significant about the answers to some of her questions. At our center we evaluated women's needs based on their answers to the questions on the forms. In addition to pregnancy options counseling, pregnancy tests, sonograms, family programs, and various classes, we also performed STI (sexually transmitted infection) testing. Part of our intake form included questions such as number of sexual partners, last date of STI testing, and results in order for us to guide clients in this area. I noted that Chloe had answered the question regarding the number of sexual partners at "over 100." This type of answer to the question frequently indicated a possibility of sex industry involvement (stripping or prostitution) or of childhood sexual abuse or both. Studies indicate that women who were sexually abused as children tend to have larger numbers of sexual partners than those who have not. The answer to this question can open a door for further inquiry and an opportunity to meet additional needs our client may have.

My experience has been that women who have experienced sexual abuse don't talk about it unless asked directly. Our client intake form consisted of a direct question, "Have you ever experienced physical, emotional, mental, or sexual abuse?" There often is a desire to tell someone about the abuse, but the victim is often just waiting for someone to care enough to ask the question. They usually send messages that are ignored by those close to them for lack of knowledge or understanding or the inability to face such a hard truth because a family member or friend often perpetrates the abuse. This was the case with Chloe. This lovely young woman, poised and confident on the exterior—sure to turn the eye of any man and induce envy in other women—was a complete mess on the inside. She was one of the walking wounded with a beautiful façade, scarred and terribly sad on the inside.

Chloe had been sexually abused as a child by a male relative. Childhood sexual abuse is usually perpetrated by a relative or close friend of the family, someone with easy access to the child that is trusted by the child and the family. This is the tragedy of childhood sexual abuse. It mars the child's entire reality and perceptions of right and wrong. It creates an alternative reality for the child that is twisted in secrets, lies, manipulation, and threats. It crushes trust and creates deep wounds. This beautiful young woman had been a victim. This victimization had led to involvement in the sex industry. She had run away from home at an incredibly early age and resorted to stripping and, ultimately, prostitution to get off the streets. It is not uncommon for stripping to escalate into prostitution as a progression of the sex trade industry. Chloe had saved her money and was able to work her way out of the industry with help from friends still working inside the industry. She had become an example for those friends of one who had actually made it out of the "life" and stayed out. She was able to go back and finish school and get a job in an office where she was currently working. This potential pregnancy was due to a "love" relationship. She was not ready for a child, though.

Chloe's pregnancy test came back negative. She was very relieved to receive the news. We scheduled her for STI (sexually transmitted infection) testing and made an appointment for her to come back for that later. I shared the Gospel with Chloe. She said it was the first time she had heard it. She was very receptive to hearing about Jesus and His love for her. Chloe broke down and showed emotion for the first time. When presented with the truth of the unconditional love of Jesus the Savior, who died on a cross for sinners, Chloe was moved to tears. I felt the love of Christ flow from me to Chloe as I shared the truth and the good news of the Gospel, and I knew that she was moved by His love for her.

A few months later, I was at a fast-food restaurant in Dallas. I looked across the restaurant, and there sat Chloe with a friend chatting and eating her lunch. She looked different—radiant, happy, innocent, pure. I wanted to approach her but did not because I did not want her to have to explain to her friend who I was.

Chloe encountered Christ the day she came into our pregnancy center. My prayer is that her name is now written in the Lamb's Book of Life, and I will see her again in eternity, pure, holy, unblemished—washed as white as snow by the blood of the Lamb—like every other soul that will be in heaven with Jesus, a precious and pure bride.

Perverted Love

This is a generation of perverted love. Love as a word is being misused and misapplied to the point of the "four-letter word" category. Bear with me as I work this out because anyone who knows me knows that my favorite saying is, "Love is the game changer."

For the sake of clarification, I am not referring to the pure and holy, transforming love of God who sent my Savior, Jesus Christ, to die on a cross for my sin. Experiencing this love transformed my life, and I live each day in the process of sanctification and will do so until I am called to step into eternity.

The love I am speaking of is a false definition of love, a cheap love as defined in our culture and within the community of believers. Cheap love coincides with cheap grace that is abounding in the community of believers. Sorry folks—it's heresy.

> *Dear friends, let us love one another, for love comes from God. Everyone who loves has been born of God and knows God. Whoever does not love does not know God, because God is love. This is how God showed his love among us; he sent his one and only son into the world that we might live through him. This is love: not that we loved God, but that he loved us and sent his son as an atoning sacrifice for our sins.*

1 John 4:7–10 (NIV)

Love does not sound cheap in that definition.

Further: in 1 John 5:2–3 (NIV) John defines proof of love for the children of God—other believers—as well as defining proof of love for God.

"This is how we know that we love the children of God: By loving God and carrying out his commands. This is love for God: to obey his commands."

Our culture does not define love in God's Holy Word—the Bible. It is not subject to twenty-first-century interpretation, including superimposing a Western worldview upon it.

Read 1 Corinthians 13.

> *Love is patient, love is kind. It does not envy, it does not boast, it is not proud. It does not dishonor others, it is not self-seeking, it is not easily angered, it keeps no record of wrongs. Love does not delight in evil but rejoices with the truth. It always protects, always trusts, always hopes, always perseveres.*
>
> 1 Corinthians 13:4–7 (NIV)

There is a difference between "God is love" and "love is God." Let's explore the difference.

"God is love" is defining part of the nature and character of God.

"Love is God" is making an idol of love as an emotion and cheapening it with a worldly, shallow, and selfish definition of love.

We have all fallen prey to this. We are inundated with it in our society of "me."

Our culture has contaminated our understanding, definition, and use of the word "love."

Most of this generation that grew up on Disney princesses and superheroes think that love is what makes a person *feel good* and that it's okay to sacrifice basic moral principles and others' rights in order to obtain such "love." But wait—that is not real love but the exact opposite of what the Bible tells us it is. That is selfishness.

Real love is like God's love as defined for us in His Word.

Let's talk about what it's not: manipulative, quid pro quo, selfish and self-seeking, cheap, harsh, unforgiving, agreement with sin, opposed to the truth.

My observation has been that when followers of Christ reject the truth that they are unprepared to receive, they often throw out the love "card" or an accusation of being judged (you are unloving because you don't agree with my sin—you are judging me). Nowhere in the Bible does it say that speaking truth is passing judgment. Neither does it say that speaking truth is not love.

Jesus spoke truth to sinners precisely *because He loved*. He always confronted people He met with truth because of love. *His motive for speaking the truth was love!*

Let's ponder this one together and meditate on it. Love is the game changer! Love is costly. Love is not defined by a fickle culture or to be used as an accusation when we don't want to hear the truth. It is not a license to sin or a cheap phrase to manipulate others to get them to agree with you or get something you want. Jesus died a criminal's death on the cross for it.

Are you willing to do the same for those you claim to love?

God is love. Love is sacrifice.

Rachel: Blinding Scales and Baby Models

Rachel came to our center for a sonogram when I was on staff as center director. Rachel knew she was pregnant and was planning to abort her child. She needed a sonogram, and to save money at the abortion clinic, she came to our center to get a free one. Rachel had an eighteen-month-old little girl named Diana. She brought Diana to the pregnancy center with her when she came for her sonogram. Diana was a beautiful little girl and was named Diana after the princess of Wales.

Rachel's demeanor was very mechanical when she arrived at the center. She was clearly showing in her pregnancy—she had a baby bump. She was reserved and unemotional as we went through the intake forms with her. She explained that she and her husband were in the country illegally; they were attempting to make money to pay an attorney to legally go through the process of obtaining citizenship. She explained how they were currently living with friends in a crowded environment with their little girl and that they just simply could not "afford" to bring another child into the world.

We counseled Rachel and explained all the options that are available to women when they are pregnant—giving birth and parenting, adoption, and abortion. We always explained that there are consequences, good or bad, to every action we take and went through some of the consequences of each option. She said she did not believe in abortion but that for financial and situational reasons, she simply could not keep this child. We shared the Gospel with Rachel, and she stated that she was a Christian. She said she knew that abortion was wrong but that she felt abortion was her only option under the circumstances. She said she knew that God would forgive her.

In Texas, at this point, there was a limitation on abortion of twenty-four weeks pregnancy. This law was changed in 2013 to twenty weeks. Our staff sonographer gave Rachel a sonogram, and she registered twenty-three weeks. This gave her one week to obtain the abortion legally in the state of Texas. The sonographer got an excellent picture of the baby on the screen. The baby was waving its arms and almost appeared to be waving hello! We were breathless in the sonogram room, praying that this woman would bond with this child through this precious picture of life. However, she remained unemotional and jumped down from the sonogram table afterward with her picture in hand to take to the abortion clinic so she could get her abortion as quickly as possible before it was too late.

At this moment, the Holy Spirit impressed upon me to show Rachel some baby models. We had a set of three-dimensional baby models in our center. They were sized from various stages of development from twelve weeks until thirty. They were life-like and soft to the touch, almost like skin. I went over and picked up the twenty-four-week model and handed it to Rachel. I told her this was close to the exact size of her baby.

She grasped it and held it and turned it over and over. She couldn't believe it. She kept asking if this was really what her baby looked like. Tears began running down her face. The emotionless exterior was beginning to crack. As she held the three-dimensional model in her hand, the physical reality of the baby inside her became real in her mind and her heart. The sonogram picture had not touched her. The sound of the heartbeat had not moved her. The waving of the little arms inside her womb during the sonogram did not evoke emotion, but the handling and the touching of a three-dimensional baby model broke her. She began sobbing. She said, "I cannot go through with this. I cannot kill my baby."

The truth was that Rachel had come from a country where she never had a biology class. She had never had a sonogram with her first child. She had no concept of egg fertilization and baby development in terms of biology and science. The reality of the three-dimensional models and what her baby looked like at this stage of development could not be denied. She had not been given this information at the abortion clinic. She had not seen pictures of baby development. When confronted with the truth, the truth set her free. The reality was her twenty-three-week-old baby was just that—a baby.

Rachel kept her child and delivered a healthy, beautiful baby girl. Months later, she came back to the center to thank us and introduce us to little Mercy. Her baby was just as beautiful as her first little girl. Rachel said that this little girl was such a blessing. She said that initially she was a little fussy and suffered from colic, but Rachel said she never minded. She was so happy that she had kept her beautiful, sweet child that the crying never bothered her. She just held her closer and loved her even more.

A few weeks later, we were able to raise enough funds to purchase Rachel and her family a double stroller so she could easily manage her two-year-old and her newborn. I delivered it to her new apartment. Her family was able to obtain their own apartment, and they no longer had to live with friends. It was a genuinely nice, safe place with plenty of room for their family. Rachel beamed as she received the stroller and proudly showed me around their home. I got to hold Mercy, and we prayed together before I left. Rachel said she knew that God had been in the midst of the encounter at the pregnancy center the day we met, and she was thankful for the baby models that had opened her eyes, removed the blinding scales, and saved her little girl that day.

> *The Lord is merciful and gracious, slow to anger, and plenteous in mercy. He will not always chide, nor will he keep his anger forever. He [has] not dealt with us after our sins; nor rewarded us according to our iniquities. For as the heaven is high above the earth, so great is his mercy toward them that fear him. As far as the east is from the west, so far [has] he removed our transgressions from us.*
>
> Psalm 103:8–12

Blessed be the name of the Lord.

My God Is a Star-Breather

My God is a star-breather. With His breath He spoke stars into existence. With His outstretched hand, He formed the earth and separated the sky from the waters. God hovered over all of it, and God "was."

I Am spoke the commandments to Moses and passed by him to reveal just a glimpse of His glory, which, by the way, was so powerful, He had to turn His back to Moses lest He kill him by the sheer magnitude of His power.

With His breath He spoke into existence the Milky Way Galaxy, the Whirlpool Galaxy (yes, He was really showing off here!), and all of space and the celestial beings. He formed the Grand Tetons, the Rocky Mountains, the Swiss Alps, and Mount Everest, the Pacific Ocean, the Indian Ocean, the Atlantic Ocean, the oceanic rift, the tectonic plates, and He said it was good, and it was.

God is the Creator, the ultimate artist, the sum of all good and the sum of all existence, and so much more. The Creator of the praying mantis, the monarch butterfly, the toucan, the flamingo, and the armadillo, the Grand Canyon, Taka Kawa Falls, the Colorado River, the Arkansas River, and the Kicking Horse, the Jungfrau, Interlaken, Lake Thune, and the seahorse.

Yet He formed me in my mother's womb, and He knew me, custom-designed me down to the number of hairs on my head. He had a plan; He broke the mold after me. Father, reveal Yourself to me! All creation shouts Your name! All creation declares Your glory!

Praise Your holy name!

The Holy One, I Am, the God of Abraham, Isaac, Jacob, and the Mediterranean Sea. The Lord God, the Lord God Almighty! The God of all creation, the Lord of all nations—He who appoints leaders and time and seasons. He who was, who is, and is to come. He who was the beginning and is the ending and who was there at the laying of the foundations of the earth. He is the God of the Shema, the tabernacle, and the temple. He is the King of kings and Lord of lords—the God of David, Daniel, Jeremiah, and Isaiah. He is the Prince of Peace, Yahweh, Adonai, and El Shaddai.

I can only fall to the ground in adoration, hard pressed, face down in Your presence, overwhelmed by Your power, amazed at Your enormity. Awestruck at Your infiniteness, overcome in the joy that You love me.

Praise Your holy name! Praise be to God! Jesus is the Lamb! Jesus is the Messiah! Jesus is the Savior!

What a wonderful plan, what perfection, ad infinitum—how wondrous. Holy, holy, holy is the Lord Almighty.

Kadosh, Kadosh, Kadosh Ata (Hebrew).

All power and praise be to His name.

Ipso facto (God is infinite in comparison to our finite nature).

"I will worship [you] toward [your] holy temple and praise [your] name for [your] lovingkindness and for [your] truth: for [you have] magnified [your] word above all [your] name."

Psalm 138:2

Weeping for Zion

I was anxious; my period was late, and I knew this was not good. Besides that, I was not feeling well. I would wake up in the morning nauseated and lethargic. The thought that I might be pregnant was inconceivable. What would my mom think? Would she be so distraught that she might attempt to take her life again? What would we do?

My mom had told me soon after her recovery and return home from the hospital after the drug overdose that she "hoped she never got to that point again." At that moment in my life, I had taken personal responsibility for her well-being, for her life. The statement itself led me to believe that it *was a possibility*. That thought terrified me. I had decided it was my job to make sure she was okay. I did everything in my power not to "rock the boat" with her. My sister had already moved out of the house, so I was in charge. I decided not to tell her.

My seventeen-year-old boyfriend decided to tell his parents. They were livid and made the decision to make an appointment for me at a Planned Parenthood clinic in Dallas, Texas. They were taking charge of the matter. They were paying for the abortion, and they did not think it prudent to tell my mother, as they knew about the suicide attempt. They told my boyfriend that he would have to work and "pay them back" for the end of the life of their grandbaby.

I felt swept away in a sea of fear and confusion with everyone else taking control of my life and telling me how things were going to be. I was too scared to do anything but go along with what the adults taking charge of my life were telling me to do. I felt powerless. It was just a couple of months before I turned sweet sixteen, and I would be old enough to go on my first "car date," and I was pregnant! My world was reeling out of control.

My first visit to the clinic was for a pregnancy test and counseling session. My test was positive, and after that news I was ill. I started zoning out during the counseling session, and the counselor seemed to be far, far away. I could barely hear her. I was having a tough time understanding her. She told me I was approximately eight weeks pregnant and that I was in the first trimester of pregnancy. I had never had a biology class, so I really didn't know what she was talking about. She told me that at this stage there was no baby yet—just a "clump of tissue" like a period. She asked me if I had any questions and what type of birth control I wanted to go on after the abortion. This question brought me back to reality and the present. I told her that I did not have any questions and that I did not need any birth control because I was never going to have sex again.

His parents scheduled the abortion, and my boyfriend escorted me to the clinic that day. The clinic was in a high-rise office building and situated just above a bar on the floor beneath it. When I arrived for my appointment, the room was full of somber-looking girls. On that day there was no one in the room who looked older than twenty years old. Some were crying quietly. My name was called, and I was sent to the back for the procedure.

The next thing I remember was lying down on a hard and cold table with a doctor at the end saying something indicative of "this won't take long." I heard the sound of a machine turning on, and it was like a loud vacuum cleaner. I looked over next to me, where there appeared to be a translucent plastic receptacle, and suddenly saw blood and tissue spattering inside of it. At that moment, I knew that they had lied to me! That was a baby! They lied to me! I killed my baby! Tears started streaming out of my eyes, but I couldn't move. I was paralyzed—unable to speak or move. I became extremely sick and passed out. The next thing I felt was the nurse come over and jab something into my arm.

I woke up in a room with other hospital beds next to me, but I was completely alone. The feeling I awoke to was one of complete and utter loss. It was an indescribable sense of loss, overwhelming sadness, and grief. It felt permanent. My baby's body had been ripped out of my body along with my soul. I had never felt so betrayed and abandoned by everyone in my life as I suffered alone in utter silence for what had just taken place. I was unable to process any of it in my fifteen-year-old mind. I would not be able to process the trauma and devastation until many, many years later.

I felt utter loss, regret, betrayal, and sadness. I was numb. I was utterly alone in the middle of the darkness—no one at my side. Not even a nurse. I glanced around and saw my clothes in a bag. I got up out of the bed and put them on. I walked groggily and shakily to the front, where a receptionist sat, and said I wanted to go. They shoved a bag at me with antibiotics and aftercare hygiene instructions and sent me on my way.

My boyfriend was there in the waiting room, looking scared to death. He jumped up and came over to assist me in walking as we left the clinic. Due to ongoing construction in the building, we had to walk through a bar that day to exit the building. I wondered how many women and girls walked through that bar after they had killed their babies. I was convinced that the clinic was evil and that they were killing babies for money as they lied to women and girls. The absurdity of women exiting through a bar after killing a baby struck me profoundly. I wouldn't cry again for a long time.

Alabaster Jar

Tears all around me—sobbing.

Perhaps real healing is going on.

Perhaps loud emotional display is to draw attention.

The crowd is loud and intense.

I am overwhelmed with the hysteria and cacophony of emotions wrought and rendered. I go to a corner and drop to my knees, head in hands.

I cover my face in the quiet place I have sought. "Lord, I have cried all my tears alone."

"No, you have not. I was there with you for each and every one, collecting them in an alabaster jar."

Oh, how You restore my soul. You alone are my peace.

You meet me in the quiet.

In the restful place of solitude, where all other voices are silenced. My Lord, my God, my King, the Holy One.

His name is Jesus.

Delilah: Delicate Flower

Delilah contacted the center by email mid-morning one day. Her email was both riveting and sad: "I had an abortion last Friday. I am terribly sad and depressed. I need to talk. No one told me I would feel this way. Can I make an appointment to come and talk?"

I immediately responded to the email. "Can you come in today? Can you be here in fifteen minutes?"

Delilah arrived at the center within an hour. She was a beautiful young woman in her mid-twenties, tall and thin, very feminine, and delicate as a flower. She had high cheekbones and deeply set, solemn, big brown eyes that were liquid, holding back many tears that were about to spill over and run down her face.

Delilah began to tell me of her life journey. She had graduated from a prestigious university in Dallas and taught German. Her parents were divorced, and both sides of her family were wealthy. Her father was a Dallas businessman; her mother was German and currently lived in Germany. Delilah had become addicted to heroin at a young age. She had been clean and sober for five years when she came into the center.

In a recovery program, she had met a young man whom she had fallen in love with quickly. They had started being sexually active within two weeks of meeting. It seemed to be a whirlwind romance initiated and consummated quickly due to mutual painful life experiences and the intense need and desire for love. Delilah became pregnant within one month of the relationship. Her boyfriend wanted her to keep the baby. Delilah was scared and confused and decided to consult her mother in Germany.

Delilah's mom suggested abortion. Delilah's mom had experienced an unplanned pregnancy in her early adult life and had decided to abort the baby. She was now recommending the same decision to her daughter an ocean away. Delilah, as many young women and girls do, trusted her mother's advice and took it against the will of the father of the baby.

My observations at the pregnancy center indicated the persons who have the most influence in an abortion decision were primarily the father of the baby or the woman's mother. It was not unusual for the influence of the mother to usurp the influence of the father of the baby in an abortion decision. This was the case for Delilah. I asked her what her mother had said about the experience of her past abortion. Delilah explained that her mother said she "never" regretted her decision.

In my eight years' experience of counseling women at the center, I doubted this claim by her mother. It can take decades for a woman to process the trauma and to realize they have been adversely affected by an abortion. It is a rare instance when a woman claims no regrets. I had not met one in eight years. Most post-abortive women profess intense emotions, such as loss, grief, sadness, and regret. As Delilah had said in her email, "No one ever told me that I would feel this way."

As we walked through Delilah's experience and she related her pain, my heart broke for her. Tears rolled down her cheeks and spilled into her lap. Her voice was quiet as a whisper, her eyes wide and soft like a doe's. She felt betrayed that no one had prepared her for the emotional trauma the abortion had wrought on her—not even her own mother.

Delilah indicated that she just wanted the pain to stop—she wanted it to go away. I asked her if she had experienced any suicidal thoughts. She admitted that she had. She insisted she just wanted the emotional pain she had been so unprepared for to stop. She explained that at the abortion center the staff had been trying to keep things "light" and "normal." She did not understand this when she was hurting so badly inside immediately after the procedure. She felt her deep pain and grief were being ignored or downplayed by the staff at the clinic.

I got to pray with Delilah with her permission. Delilah told me she did not believe in Jesus Christ and was wary of those who claimed to be Christians. She had formerly explored spiritualism and new-age practices. However, she allowed me to pray for her in the name of Jesus. In our center we shared the Gospel with every woman and girl who allowed us to. I asked her if I could share with her what I believed. She allowed me to present the Gospel message and took home a Bible and a pamphlet explaining what it meant to be a Christ follower.

I asked Delilah to do me one favor—when asked by others, she should tell the truth about how the abortion made her feel. The fact that women are not telling the truth of the pain it has caused allows other women to find out too late. It is time that women are honest with each other. The reality is that abortion is painful physically, spiritually, emotionally, and psychologically. Women need to be prepared for the onslaught of loss, sorrow, regret, and grief. I connected Delilah with an organization that provided one-on-one counseling for post-abortive women. Many post-abortive group-healing programs will not accept a client until at least one year post-abortion. I knew Delilah needed help sooner rather than later.

I was able to get her an appointment within the week to meet one on one with a professional counselor who specialized in post-abortive women. Through that counseling connection, Delilah later went through a group abortion recovery program that helped her to cope with her loss and to realize she was not alone.

Over the next year, Delilah began attending church with her boyfriend and became a Christ follower. They were married in August of 2013, and I was invited to attend their wedding. Sadly, their marriage broke up about a year later. Approximately 80 percent of relationships dissolve after an abortion. However, Delilah is thriving now and is working on a master's program in social work while continuing to teach German lessons and travel the world. She has a new special man friend in her life. She remains a delicate and fragile flower, one whom the Creator knew before the foundations of the world. She is a delicate and beautiful flower that touched my soul forever with her deep pain and sense of betrayal but the ultimate desire to embrace a new life in the freedom of truth and forgiveness.

Praise the Lord.

Holocaust: Ponder This

Yesterday I went to the Holocaust Museum in Dallas. It was a riveting and frightening reminder of how quickly things can go bad. How rapidly evil can extend its talons and infiltrate, darken, and consume an entire culture (*kultur*, as the Germans referred to it).

Ponder this printed on WWII posters: "How well are you sleeping? Is there something you could have done to save millions of innocent people—men, women, and children—from torture and death?" Or "This is strictly a race against death! Is there something you could have done to save millions of innocent people—men, women, and children—from torture and death?"

Did you sleep well last night, or are you asleep all the time? Complacency truly does equate to complicity. The reason evil prevails when it does is that good people stand by and do nothing.

What do you do when you become aware of injustice? Thank God it is not directed toward you? What do you do when you observe evil? Turn your head and think to yourself it is not your problem? What would you have done standing in that church when the trains rolled by with railcars packed to overflow with human flesh chugging toward the death camps and human incinerators? Sing louder? Tell yourself what a great human being you are because you attend church and this does not affect you? Until when?

The Dallas Morning News headlines on April 19, 1943, read, "Allies Sink Axis Ship, Damage 5, Down 38 Planes." Directly beneath it ran the headline of a Hollywood actress who had eloped with her manager twice her age. Do we see the press trying to avert our attention today to the absurd, ridiculous, and irrelevant from injustice, horrors on humanity, and countries imploding? Is this a tactic to divert the public who couldn't possibly handle the truth of the current state of the world?

We are on dangerous ground in the United States of America. One of the Jewish holocaust survivors spoke of how she wanted to kiss the ground when she landed on American shores. Would she feel that welcome today? Would she feel the same about America?

This is a country where most people go to sleep every night ignoring the ignition of evil around the globe primarily because they are ignoring it in their own backyard. Our culture is in a state so close to that of the Nazis in Germany when Hitler came on scene that it is chilling.

Most Americans are asleep. They are worrying about what college their child is going to attend, what new car is next on the list, where their new mansion is going to be located, and what destination their next vacation will be.

In the meantime, we are approaching ten times the holocaust (that is close to sixty million) babies aborted since Roe v. Wade legislation passed in 1973. Let that sink in.

People yawn when you bring it up. People snore when you talk about the number of civilians killed in Syria or the number of civilians killed because of the Muslim Brotherhood in Egypt.

I cannot ignore the condition of the ancient Israelites before they lost their nation as described in the Old Testament. They were described as apathetic and complacent, unconcerned about the poor—particularly the orphans and widows—going through the routines of worship insincerely (their hearts weren't in it), and sacrificing their children to the God of Moloch.

Sounds a lot like our society, which is sacrificing our children by abortion to the God of convenience. We have more beautiful megachurches than ever before, packed with people who are not making a difference in our culture. You tell me why. More money has been poured into buildings than the GDP of the majority of countries that currently exist on our planet. We are guilty as a nation of the same things the ancient Israelites were, while most people are either asleep or sleeping well.

During Hitler's reign good people who professed to love God and follow the Christian faith stood by and did nothing while millions of men, women, and children faced certain atrocities and death because they were immobilized by either apathy and complacency or fear. Some things are worth dying for. Are you sleeping well these days, or are you just asleep? It's time we ponder this with eyes wide open.

Lord, awaken Your church.

"And the Dragon Stood on the Shore of the Sea"

"The dragon stood on the shore of the sea. And I saw a beast coming out of the sea. It had ten horns and seven heads, with ten crowns on its horns, and on each head a blasphemous name" (Revelation 13:1, NIV).

The dragon is biding its time as the seas churn and the lands start to burn. Plagues are unleashing. Bombs are screeching.

The blood of babies killed in the womb crying from the ground, not unnoticed by the Holy One.

Crystals charming, witchcraft practiced openly, idolatry abounding while our nation entertains itself.

Complacency and apathy are the desserts of the day.

Some who claim Christianity say, "I no longer believe in Satan or a literal hell." Assertions such as, "Everyone has their own truth."

There is nothing new under the sun. Sin repackaged, that is all.

Internet porn is destroying an entire generation. Sex trafficking is a multibillion business. Pedophilia is rampant.

The volcanoes are boiling. And the smoke is rising up to heaven. And the dragon stands on the shore of the sea—watch and see.

In a robe dipped in blood comes the Righteous One; on a warhorse, He draws nigh.

LeAnn, the Liar

On the day I walked into Planned Parenthood as a fifteen-year-old girl to have an abortion, I planned to lie about my age. I was going to tell them that I was sixteen years old. For some reason, in my mind, that age sounded more appropriate to be involved in sexual activity, which in my case, had manifested itself in an unplanned pregnancy. It didn't matter because they did not ask me for any type of identification or proof of age anyway at the clinic.

The fact that this thought even crossed my mind at age fifteen reflected the *shame* that I felt. Shame and lying go hand in hand. The shame of abandonment, rejection, feeling unloved, and desperately seeking anything to fill the need for love ultimately surfaced in a lie about my age that would lead to a false identity that would keep me in bondage for many years.

About a year after the abortion, my older sister spotted my boyfriend and me at a local lake where teens went to cruise on weekends and busted me. Teenagers cruised around the lake to show off their cars, blare their music, and drive around and around the same route engaging with others in car or other talk. Drinking alcohol of one kind or another was part of the cruise scene. Sometimes it included smoking pot. There was beer in my boyfriend's car, and we were both definitely underage.

The result of this chance encounter with my sister and her boyfriend, who were doing the same thing at the time, resulted in her telling my mother about seeing us there, which resulted in my being grounded for one month. In an attempt to get out of the punishment and out of the house, I wrote my mother a letter of apology and signed it "LeAnn, the liar" because I had lied about where I was going that day.

My mother saved this letter, and for some reason it was a source of amusement to my entire family even years later in mature adulthood. At family gatherings it was occasionally brought out, much to my chagrin, and I would endure endless chants of "LeAnn, the liar." The problem is that this was mean-spirited in nature, and sometimes it made me angry. I had not learned to draw boundaries with people as a young person, as I did not believe I was worthy, valuable, or deserving of honor or respect. I was not good at it as an adult until after I came to Christ, and He started teaching me how to set boundaries. There were certain responsibilities He wanted to entrust to me, but He could not do so until I learned to set proper boundaries with people that reinforced my own dignity as His daughter.

One time after such an incident occurred years later in adulthood, I saw a friend of mine, who speaks Arabic, the next day. When my friend greeted me, she referred to me with an Arabic term of endearment meaning "beloved one." I noted the contrast in the hurtful treatment of my biological family, and this dear sister in Christ and I could not understand why my family had such a tough time loving me like she did. My family seemed to thrive on sarcasm and criticism. It was like itching ears could not wait to hear unwelcome news about one another. Support, encouragement, and honoring one another were foreign concepts. After I became a believer, I spent time in prayer over the mean-spiritedness of the "LeAnn, the liar" letter that seemed to never go away that was so hurtful to me. It was like a constant reminder to me of my past. Salt in the wound poured out for the pleasure and amusement of others.

Then the Lord brought to remembrance the untruth I intended to tell about my age at the abortion clinic. I thought about the shame wrapped up in that lie and all that it implied. I thought about how I myself had intended to falsely identify myself, to misrepresent my age. I myself had penned the apology letter with the title of that false identity.

I was guilty of lying, but that was not *who* I was. Neither was I identified as the "girl who had the abortion." Abortion did not identify me. Shame was heaped upon shame.

The Lord lovingly impressed upon me that this was a false identity that had been placed on me as a fifteen-year-old girl, an identity that the enemy had tried to propagate throughout my entire life and keep me paralyzed in shame. An identity that was redeemed through the blood of the Lamb—Jesus—shed for all of us on a cross. The Lord lovingly reminded me that my identity is in Christ alone. When God looks at me, He sees Christ, my kinsman redeemer. He sees me as lovely, pure, and righteous—purchased—by the blood of the Lamb.

LeAnn the liar, LeAnn the least likely, was now LeAnn the *loved*, pursued, won, and treasured by the Righteous One—the Lord not only of the here and now and the come what may but also the Lord of my past. LeAnn, created to speak truth.

Blessed be the name of the Lord.

Across Deep Rivers

Lord, let the deep rivers rush through my soul-crushing false foundations and false identities—those I have assumed and those placed on me by others—removing the debris of the consequences of sin (mine and those who have sinned against me), cleansing, renewing, redeeming, recreating, sanctifying me without the river crushing me.

Restore to me ten times what the locust eaters have taken.

Let the living water have His way with me. Let it be for me as You have said.

Let the power of the living water ignite the Spirit's fire deep down in my soul, and let it burn! Your Spirit's fire is in me; Your Spirit's fire goes before me. I am a watchman on the wall! The same power that formed the valleys between the mountain ranges—that same unfathomable power—is living inside of me! I have the Spirit of the living God inside of me! Thank You, Jesus!

I will cross deep rivers because You are with me.

Belinda: A Tortured Soul

Belinda was one of my best friends in high school, especially for the last two years. Belinda and I ran the streets of our hometown, a suburb of Dallas. We worked hard, played hard, and spent lots of time with boys. Belinda's goal in life was to get married to her boyfriend. My goal was never to get married. As fate would have it, I got married before she did, at age eighteen.

She was from a troubled family. Her father was an alcoholic who was abusive to her mother when he drank. His personality was like Dr. Jekyll and Mr. Hyde. An otherwise seemingly gentle giant and quiet man became a raving, abusive maniac after a couple of drinks. He would routinely throw suppers across the table that his wife had carefully prepared due to small infractions, such as not being salty enough to suit his taste.

Belinda loved her family and had especially taken on the role of protector of her mother. If we had plans to cruise around town and her father began to drink, she would not leave her mother alone with him. She felt at age sixteen that it was her responsibility to make sure nothing "bad" happened if it was at all in her power to do so. This struck a chord with me, as we shared this commonality in our lives. If Belinda's father was at work and she felt secure leaving her mother at the house alone, we would be inseparable.

Shortly after high school, Belinda and her parents moved about fifty miles away from the Dallas area. I moved to a small town on the Texas coast near Beaumont, south of Houston. We seemed to lose touch for a few years until I moved back to the Dallas area, and we were reacquainted. During this time, I learned that Belinda had become bulimic. At the time, there was no name for this disease, and eating disorders were not readily recognized, as awareness was not common. She described to me her symptoms and the fact that she felt like the "devil" was telling her to eat and purge and that she had no control over the impulses whatsoever.

After that I learned that she and her sister had visited a psychic. The psychic told her that someone close to her was going to die very soon. Belinda was terribly upset and thought it might be her mother (at the hand of her father) and phoned me to tell me about it. I was horrified that she had visited a psychic. Even though I knew nothing about what a psychic did, believed, or practiced—that indeed is witchcraft—something inside me knew they were sad news.

Two weeks later, at age twenty-two, my best friend from high school and early adulthood died after being shot in the back at a phone booth near her small town. She was on the phone talking to her mother at the time, checking in with her to make sure she was okay while Belinda was out on a date. She lived for a few days in the hospital prior to dying from her injury. My life seemed to be a series of pain and crushing losses.

Ling Sings: The Mystery of God

We approached the waiting room and opened the door to call the next client. My eyes scanned the waiting room as I wondered which client was next and would be ours. Ling stood up and walked toward the open door. I was shocked. I thought that she was a young man.

I walked into the counseling room as an observer. I was visiting a pregnancy center in another city to review their client systems. I was relaxed and enjoying the role of a mere observer. The counselor took charge. I was in the backseat on this one.

Ling had short black hair with a male-styled haircut. She wore no makeup and was dressed in men's clothes. She had solid square shoulders and carried herself in the masculine. She wore neither jewelry nor any adornments of femininity. Ling was at the center for a pregnancy test. She was in a relationship with her manager at a pizza shop.

Ling began unpacking her past. Her life story contained sexual abuse, lesbianism, gang rape with objects, rejection by her family, and hospitalization for mental issues. She was barely twenty years old.

Through the unpacking process, she developed a rapport with her counselor and told us that she was a songwriter and a singer and asked if she could sing us a song she had written. Of course, we said sure but were a little skeptical. We were still processing the details of her life story, inundated by brutality, abuse, and rejection. My heart cried out in anguish for her, for the evil perpetrated against her, for the injustices she had endured. I grieved for this poor, tortured soul. And then Ling opened her mouth to sing.

The most beautiful, feminine, angelic voice I had ever heard proceeded from her mouth. It was sweet, captivating, other-worldly, breathtaking. The counselor and I were stunned; we were speechless, unable to take our eyes off her or to turn away from that heavenly voice that proceeded from this most unlikely form. The words were her heart, written on her soul, pouring out from her mouth. We were sponges soaking up the message, receiving the rivers of the Spirit of God flowing from her lips.

The room was thick with His divine presence, and time had been suspended as Ling poured out her heart with the loveliest voice I had ever heard then or have heard since. I looked into Ling's face and knew we had just received a glimpse of God through the voice of this unlikely girl.

The Spirit of God had just manifested in the midst of us as she sang mostly with her eyes closed. Our eyes were wide open. I was frozen, afraid to move, afraid I would miss one moment of this divine manifestation of the Spirit of God. His presence was heavy in the room. Her voice was pure beauty; her countenance was lovely. I was breathless—afraid to breathe and disturb the movement occurring in the Spirit. She smiled the entire time she sang.

Then the moment was over. Ling opened her eyes. The smile was gone, and her face expressionless.

The counselor and I were reeling, fully aware that we had just experienced the divine presence of God. We had just been given a glimpse into the love of God for Ling, the beauty He chose to manifest through her. We knew full well that our God could manifest Himself however He chose through whomever He chose. He specializes in the least likely and delights in shattering our preconceived notions of Him. He is not subject to the limitations that humanity places on Him—for an infinite God cannot be contained nor absolutely defined by mere humans. He will pour out His Spirit on whomever He chooses and in any way He pleases. All glory belongs to Him.

Ling cried when she received the news that her test was negative. She was hoping for a baby to love.

My previous understanding of the Holy Spirit, limited by my own finite thinking, had been shattered in a moment by the angelic voice of an unlikely girl. God placed in her a beautiful voice, a gift of His love, for Ling, whom He purposed ultimately for His glory.

My God does not have to conform to my limited human thinking, preferring to create beauty and manifest His presence whenever and however He chooses...through human beings created in His image to glorify His great name! I am so grateful that my thoughts cannot capture Him and that my heart cannot contain Him.

Blessed be the name of the Lord.

Your Dad Has Shot Himself

It was approximately 8:00 a.m. on a Saturday, July 6, 2002, and I had just put on a pot of coffee to enjoy when the phone rang at my house in Garland, Texas. On the end of the line was my uncle Bill—whom I rarely spoke to—calling me from my father's house. "LeAnn, this is your uncle Bill; I'm afraid your father has shot himself." What? How could that be possible?

I said, "Is he okay? Where is he? How is he doing?" Uncle Bill hesitated but only for a moment. "I'm afraid he's dead." Some sort of bizarre, automated response retorted from my body, proceeded from my mouth, "Well, where is he?" Uncle Bill answered that he was out in his workshop/office at the back of his property and that the ambulance was on its way. However, he had stopped breathing and was clearly dead. Uncle Bill said that my father had shot himself in the chest with a deer rifle.

I dropped the phone on the tile floor in my kitchen. It broke into about three pieces as it smashed onto the tile floor. I remember going into some sort of weird sensory-heightened response where every sight, sound, and smell was accentuated. The coffee brewing on the counter smelled a hundred times stronger than usual. The sound of the phone as it crashed on the floor sounded like a bomb going off. The brightness of the sun shining through the windows was eye scorching. I had a bad dream the night before and was recalling it detail by detail; for some reason it was playing and replaying loudly like a movie in my mind. I began to sob like I had never sobbed before. I had awakened that morning with a troubled spirit.

I went into my oldest son's room, age sixteen at the time, and woke him with the news. "Papa Buck is dead."

I then went into my younger son's room, age ten at the time, woke him, and told him the same. I was still crying unrestrainedly. It seemed, for some reason, this would be easier news to deliver raw and uncut—easier to make it believable, easier to get all the sordid details and flooding emotions out on the table. They asked me if he had had a heart attack; I said no and told them the truth. He had shot himself in the chest with a deer rifle that my brother had given him as a Father's Day gift. We all cried.

I got dressed and went over to my father's house. I insisted on going out into his workshop/office and seeing the scene. That was a mistake. There were blood splatters on the wall of his office. Pictures of his grandchildren were splattered with his own blood. He had supposedly shot himself while sitting down in his office chair, leaning up against his desk.

According to the police officer's reenactment of the scene, after the shot was fired, he had stood up and walked into the entranceway of his office and collapsed. That was where I spotted a piece of his heart still lying on the floor. I saw the bullet hole in the wall where the bullet had gone through his body and then through a wall behind him. It was a powerful rifle and a large caliber bullet. My father was a man small in stature. I could not figure out how he could have shot himself in the chest with that rifle. There was no suicide note.

Many days during the aftermath, I would cry alone in my shower so the boys could not hear me. I would just cry and cry, "My daddy, my daddy." Long since divorced and remarried, my mother was not particularly empathetic regarding my father's death. She left town the day after we buried him. It felt somehow like I was abandoned all over again by both of them. I just tried to concentrate on my boys and to try and help them make sense of such a senseless, horrific act.

Toward the end of his life, my father, who had actually married and remarried numerous times after he left us, made a sincere effort to have a relationship with his adult children and with his grandchildren. He loved his grandchildren deeply.

I remember one day when he called me and spoke to me about my oldest son, Chad. He was marveling about the smart, funny, sweet kid he was after having recently spent time with him. He began to cry on the phone as he talked about how much he loved Chad.

There were mysterious circumstances concerning my father's death. There were questions because my stepmother had waited thirty minutes to call 911 emergency for help. She had taken the time to have a shower after she had bloodied her nightgown after hearing the shot and discovering his body. The Garland Police Department was adamant it was a suicide. His death certificate reflected the cause of death as "suicide" accordingly.

I had a dream many years later that my father had not committed suicide and that my stepmother had hired someone to kill my father and make it look like a suicide. His death remains a mystery.

"[You are] my hiding place; [you will] preserve me from trouble; [you will] compass me about with songs of deliverance. Selah."

Psalm 32:7

Out of the depths have I cried unto you, O LORD. Lord, hear my voice: let your ears be attentive to the voice of my supplications. If you, LORD, should mark iniquities, O Lord, who shall stand? But there is forgiveness with you, that you may be feared. I wait for the LORD, my soul does wait, and in his word do, I hope. My soul waits for the Lord more than they that watch for the morning; I say more than they that watch for the morning.

Psalm 130:1–6

Steady on Love, I'll Make You a Cup of Tea

The pain was physically tangible. It was like crawling across broken glass naked. I wanted to cry but could not. It was like crying was the acknowledgment of reality. I saved the crying for later.

It came in my bed at night along with some sort of deep wailing noise that came from somewhere deep inside of me, a sound I didn't immediately recognize as coming from me. Sometimes it came in the shower with the noise of the water drowning it out.

I ached in a place that no one could touch. No human being has the capacity to reach into such depths of despair. Solitude is easier than company. You do not have to pretend or feign niceties. It is in the place of aloneness that the deep feelings of grief can process. No other human can comfort in that place. No judgment, no frivolity, no assumption, no presumption allowed. It is necessary so the grief can flow out unhindered.

I am not strong. In that place, You are with me, holding me in pure love, enveloping me in Your presence. You are the only One who has ever properly held my heart. You are the only One I trust with it. I am Yours, and You are mine. I am safe with You. I am not at all alone!

I just want to be alone to grieve in my own way—to pour my heart out to You. Humans, please pretend I am invisible and by no means ask anything from me! How selfish of you to request anything of me! How dare you make judgment calls or try and quantify my grief?

Have you walked in my shoes? Have you crawled across a battlefield ridden with mines and broken glass and survived? Have you had parts of your family and friends blown up along the way?

What have you given up? Who has stolen from you? What have you sacrificed? Whom have you loved? For whom would you have given your life? What cross have you carried? What pain is it that you have endured? What love have you buried?

It seems strange that loss and grief enhance our capacity for life and love! Once you are on the other side of the grief, it causes you to hold loved ones dearer—to be open to give and to receive love. It is facing your worst fears head-on and surviving and daring to love and to receive love again.

To love with wild abandon, fearlessly and intensely. Wild at heart, a heart's adventure!

But do not rush me to the other side. This one walks at her own pace. This grief must be walked through. This one loves deeply; these are not shallow waters. Assumptions and judgments are pathetically near-sighted and shallow, or have you not yet ventured into the deep waters?

Lord, let the deep waters rush over my head. I know You are with me, and I trust You implicitly. You are the very breath of my life! To You alone do I turn my face!

> *Depart from me [you] workers of iniquity; for the Lord [has] heard the voice of my weeping. The Lord [has] heard my supplication; The Lord will receive my prayer.*

*Let all my enemies be ashamed and sore vexed; let them
return and be ashamed suddenly.*

Psalm 6:8–10

What a simple kindness, never to be forgotten, a lovely cup of tea
poured out in a gesture of love, kindness, and simplicity.

Blessed be the name of the Lord.

*I love the LORD, because he [has] heard my voice and my
supplications. Because he [has] inclined his ear unto me,
therefore will I call upon him as long as I live. The sorrows
of death compassed me, and the pains of hell [got] hold upon
me: I found trouble and sorrow. Then called I upon the
name of the LORD: O LORD, I beseech [you], deliver my
soul. Gracious is the LORD, and righteous; [yes], our God
is merciful. The LORD [preserves] the simple: I was brought
low, and he helped me. Return unto [your] rest, O my soul;
for the LORD [has] dealt bountifully with [you].*

*For [you have] delivered my soul from death, [my] eyes from
tears, and my feet from failing. I will walk before the LORD
in the land of the living. I believed therefore have I spoken.
I was greatly afflicted. I said in my haste, all men are liars.
What shall I render unto the LORD for all his benefits toward me? I will take the cup of salvation and call upon the
name of the LORD. I will pay my vows unto the LORD
now in the presence of all his people. Precious in the sight of
the LORD is the death of his saints. O LORD, truly I am
[your] servant; I am [your] servant, and the son of [your]*

handmaid: [you have] loosed my bonds. I will offer to [you]
the sacrifice of thanksgiving and will call upon the name of
the LORD. I will pay my vows unto the LORD now in the
presence of all his people. In the courts of the LORD's house,
in the midst of [you], O Jerusalem. Praise [you] the LORD.

Psalm 116

Ariel: Daughter of Zion

Ariel walked into the center looking like a 1940s-era model. She was a striking woman in her early thirties. She was impeccably dressed and had an air of elegance and superiority about her. However, I looked into her eyes and could see that she was completely broken. The other stuff (the outward appearance and attitude) were coping mechanisms to try and divert or hide the absolute brokenness of this young woman. My immediate impression before she spoke a word to me was that she had been raped.

She completed her paperwork efficiently and quickly and took a seat while she waited to be called back for counseling. I perused her paperwork and noted some of her answers to questions that would need some critical time during our session. I also noted that she had left blank many of the questions on the sexual health questionnaire. I called her back to talk, and she began to unload the details of her life and the situation that had brought her to the center.

Ariel was a professional sex worker. She had just returned from Beverly Hills, where she worked as a high-priced escort. In fact, she had plastic surgery to make her look more like a Hollywood actor than she once had looked. She was very well "done." She, unfortunately, had suffered abuse repeatedly from an incredibly early age. Ariel ran away from home at age fifteen due to sexual abuse by her mother's boyfriend. Her mother professed to be a witch. Ariel did not really believe in the occult, and she found it quite difficult to have any type of relationship with her mother, who lived in Dallas.

The most recent trauma in Ariel's life was that she had been raped by her pimp and became pregnant. Ariel had women's health issues due to past sexual abuse of her body. She had been told that she would most likely not be able to carry the baby due to these issues and was advised to have an abortion by a medical doctor. Her pimp, back in California, had kicked her out. Her mother wanted her to have an abortion too. She did not want to be responsible for Ariel and her grandbaby. Ariel wanted to keep the baby. She said she had always wanted something of her own to love.

We confirmed by our own pregnancy test that she was most certainly pregnant and was right at twenty-one weeks on her first visit. She was very tiny and barely showing. She was looking for support and resources from us since she no longer had a source of income. We counseled Ariel about parenting and adoption and the pros and cons of both these options. Ariel was clear that she would never consider abortion or adoption as options. She wanted this baby more than she had ever wanted anything in her life.

We asked a series of questions to qualify her for placement in one of the maternity homes we worked with. It was discovered that she was being treated for bipolar disorder and that this would disqualify her from most of the group homes. However, we still had a couple of possibilities for her in terms of an extended stay in case her mother kicked her out of the house.

A few weeks later, Ariel came into the center with an exceptionally large leather brief stuffed to the brim with paper. When I greeted her at the door, I knew something was terribly wrong. By this time

Ariel had a baby bump, was a little disheveled (compared to her prior glamorous appearance), and her face was quite terse and white. I asked her to come and sit on the sofa in the reception room and sat down on the cushion beside her and asked what we could do to help.

Ariel, without a word, systematically took hold of the papers in her leather brief and, one by one, began tossing them in my face. She used foul language to describe each paper as they flew toward my face. I was quite taken aback and caught them in my own hand to divert them.

"Ariel," I said, "please don't throw papers in my face. I can't help you when you are throwing papers in my face." I spoke the words with a calmness and deliberateness that could only come from the Holy Spirit. I was in no way angry at her. In fact, as I looked at this poor, wretched, abused, overwhelmed young woman, I felt only love for her. I knew the hurt inside her was driving her actions.

She stopped. I said, "Let us pick these up and sort them out. I will help you complete these papers." The papers were required for various disabilities and benefits for which she had been deemed eligible. She needed to complete them all to receive the benefits available to her. I could completely understand why she felt overwhelmed. I was not pregnant, recovering from abuse, or on the brink of being homeless, and the sheer volume of the paperwork overwhelmed me!

For about two weeks, every day, Ariel would come at lunchtime, and we would enjoy a light lunch while I helped her to complete the paperwork. During this time, Ariel, who was Jewish, allowed me to start praying for her in Jesus' name. I shared the Gospel with her. I prayed that the truth of the Word of God would permeate her heart, mind, soul, and spirit. I knew God had plans for this resilient young woman!

Several months later, unexpectedly, I received a text from Ariel. She let me know that she had moved to Israel and had given birth to a healthy baby boy there! Mother and son were both doing very well. She was surrounded with relatives there willing to help her and her son. She need never return to her mother's home, her former way of life, or her abusive pimp. She was full of hope and joy. I thought about the goodness of God and how amazing that He provided Ariel, the least likely in the eyes of the world, the opportunity to go to Israel and give birth to hope in the form of a son.

Blessed be the name of the Lord.

"Teach me [your] way, O LORD; I will walk in [your] truth: unite my heart to fear [your] name. I will praise [you], O LORD my God with all my heart; and I will glorify [your] name forever more."

Psalm 86:11–12

"Better is the end of a thing than the beginning thereof; and the patient in spirit is better than the proud in spirit."

Ecclesiastes 7:8

The Flight

I walked up the mountain with a stick in my hand.

It was a walking stick, which doubled as a weapon in case a wild animal, snake, or spider should cross my path.

For some reason, it felt so light in my hands.

The journey was challenging, but there was beauty along the way.

The path was steep and winding; the ground was uneven, and the rocks slippery.

At times, there were boulders to maneuver around; giant conglomerates of sediment formed and cast under high pressure and shaped by running water and sediment over much time. "Minerals," as my geology teacher used to say.

Sometimes they looked impossible to surmount; at times, I glanced back at the path I had just walked and thought I might have to turn back. But only a fleeting thought as a voice whispered in my ear, "Keep going. I am with you on this journey; I have something for you on this road."

I continued up the path around the boulders.

I noted as I reached the higher elevation that the view had changed. It became clearer and more beautiful. The sky was crisp and deep blue; the clouds were pure white and had more depth and character; the sun shone like a beacon from a lighthouse piercing every corner of the sky, illuminating the challenging paths below, casting a beautiful array of light prisms on the magnificent beauty at the top.

At the top, where the view was breathtaking, I sucked air into my lungs and held it there, enjoying how good the clean mountain oxygen felt inside.

I gazed over the tops of tall evergreens, brushing the bottom of the horizon as I stared out to the place where earth meets sky.

That's when the image of the bird caught the corner of my eye, and I turned to enjoy watching her flight.

It was a large hawk flying ever so gracefully across my line of sight. Her wings dipped ever so effortlessly down and up just enough to sustain her altitude and continue her flight.

She suddenly soared upward at a great speed as if to show off her strength and skills or maybe just to enjoy them!

Then she zigzagged back and forth, up and down, in a beautiful solo dance with the endless sky. Finally, she flew gracefully away out of my sight and on with her own journey.

I was thinking about how beautiful the bird was and pondering her amazing flight when, out of the corner of my right eye, I caught a glimpse of another hawk, flying fast and strong across the sky in pursuit—intention in every movement of his wings and in every upward and downward direction of his flight.

Suddenly, the other hawk reappeared in the sky! The two flew in perfect unison, circling twice in a secret dance right in front of my line of sight.

It was a beautiful dance wrought in perfect peace and grace...in pure beauty, strength, unison, and freedom.

And then they were gone! Off to continue their flight, their journey of life. The message was not lost on me.

I stood in awe of YHWH and His goodness on the side of that mountain. Blessed be the name of the Lord.

Alice Cooper in Tulsa

It was an October day in 2003. It had been a nice short flight on Southwest Airlines from Dallas, Texas, to Tulsa, Oklahoma. I was visiting a long-time insurance client who specialized in the oil and gas industry in Oklahoma. This client looked a little like John Denver from the 1970s but with a rock and roll twist. He was quite the character and loved a variety of music. His treat that evening was an Alice Cooper concert at the Tulsa Convention Center.

I was in my hotel room getting ready for the concert when my cell phone rang. I looked down at the number and knew it was my hematologist oncologist, a blood cancer doctor, and thought to myself, *This must be bad; she's calling me in the evening.* My stomach took a little dip as I answered.

I had become ill with various symptoms in early 2003—about six months after my father's death. These symptoms led to a whole series of doctors and medical tests. I was quite sure I had given enough vials of blood to stock a blood bank for a week. During this time, I worked continually at my job as a commercial insurance broker. I first received the news that I might have cancer while driving across Lake Pontchartrain in Louisiana when my doctor called.

The doctor said I needed to return to Dallas immediately. His office made a referral for me to see a hematologist oncologist.

I put the unfamiliar words together and figured out what that meant. "You think that I have cancer, don't you?" They would not answer the question—just said to get back to Dallas immediately. I politely told them I would return after my business trip as scheduled.

The doctors had diagnosed me with a type of bone marrow cancer for which there was no treatment. Something inside of me rejected that diagnosis completely. I did not ever believe that I had cancer. Even when I entered the fancy oncology building at UTSW (University of Texas Southwestern Medical Center) with its beautifully colored blown glass sculptures, I did not agree with it. When I entered the waiting room full of people who were clearly ill, fragile, and ashen, some with IVs rigged up even in the waiting room, I knew I did not have this disease, and I told people so. They thought I was in denial. After all, the doctor had already given me pamphlets on how to die with dignity by doing yoga, how to tell your children you were going to die, and how to craft a will.

The only moment of doubt was the moment my cell phone rang in Tulsa, Oklahoma, at about seven thirty in the evening while I was preparing to go out for an Alice Cooper concert with my colleague and our client.

"Hello, LeAnn. I am sorry to bother you in the evening." I had been waiting ten days for the results to be staged by Mayo Clinic, where many vials of my blood had been sent. Staging meant basically to tell me how long I had to live.

"LeAnn, I have the best news for you. I am sorry it took so long, but I had Mayo double-check all the results, as I have never seen anything like this before. There is no evidence of cancer. It is like a miracle."

My oncologist was a lovely, kind Jewish woman. She was the most gentle and empathetic doctor I had ever encountered. I was speechless. It was then that I realized buried deep down inside of me, I must have had a tiny doubt as a flood of relief came over me.

All I could manage to say was, "Thank you for calling, doctor." She explained she would be referring me to another specialty doctor, a rheumatologist, which is a specialized internal medicine doctor. I hung up the phone.

Just as I hung up the phone, the Spirit of God moved in my hotel room at the DoubleTree Hotel in Tulsa. I heard a voice in my spirit that said, "Go and get the Bible out of that nightstand." I surreptitiously walked over to the nightstand and opened it. Inside was a Gideon's Bible. I picked it up and pulled it out. "Now open it." I opened up the Bible, and there was Psalm 38.

"Now read it." I began reading, and Psalm 38 read:

A Psalm of David to bring to remembrance.

O LORD, rebuke me not in [your] wrath; neither chasten me in [your] hot displeasure. For [your] arrows stick fast in me, and [your] hand [presses] me sore.

There is no soundness in my flesh because of [your] anger; neither is there any rest in my bones because of my sin.

For [my] iniquities are gone over [my] head as a heavy burden they are too heavy for me.

I am troubled; I am bowed down greatly; I go mourning all the daylong.

For my loins are filled with a loathsome disease; and there is no soundness in my flesh. I am feeble and sorely broken. I roared because of the disquietness of my heart. Lord, all my desire is before [you]; and my groaning is not hidden from [you].

My heart [pants], my strength [fails] me; as for the light of [my] eyes, it also is gone from me. My lovers and my friends stand aloof from my sore; and my kinsmen stand far off.

They also that seek after my life lay snares for me: and they that seek my hurt speak mischievous things, and imagine deceits all the daylong.

But I, as a deaf man, heard not; and I was as a dumb man that [opens] not his mouth. Thus, I was as a man that [hears] not, and in whose mouth are no reproofs.

For in [you], O LORD, do I hope [you will] hear, O Lord my God.

For I said, hear me, or else otherwise they should rejoice over me: when my foot [slips], they magnify themselves against me.

For I will declare my iniquity: I will be sorry for my sin.

But [my] enemies are lively, and they are strong: and they that hate me wrongfully are multiplied. They also that render evil for good are my adversaries; because I follow the thing that good is. Forsake me not, O LORD: O my God, be not far from me.

Make haste to help me, O Lord my salvation.

In that very moment, I had several thoughts that bombarded my mind at once: *God is real!*

I was a sinner, and I was sorry! God had saved me!

It's hard to describe how all the understanding came at once. I knew that I was a sinner; I was convicted and knew that I was "sick" because of sin and that God had saved me from this sin sickness: the "sickness in my bones"—on purpose for a purpose, His purpose.

Immediately after this instant of understanding and my realization that I was really a sinner and deserved death, but clearly God had saved me, He did the most amazing and beautiful thing ever. It was like He took a vial of unconditional love and poured it out over my head to overflow and cascade down my entire body. I was completely awash and enveloped in His pure, unconditional love—something I had never experienced before. I relished the experience as tears fell from my eyes. I wanted the moment never to end, to stay there in that perfect and pure love, perfect peace, and perfect *purity* forever.

The Spirit of God moved in that room and led me to the Word of God and the Spirit, and the Word cut even unto "joints and marrow." My life changed forever. The love of God transformed me!

I grabbed a pen and stationery from the bedside table of the DoubleTree Hotel in Tulsa, Oklahoma, and I wrote, "My life has changed forever. From this day forward, I will live every day for God! I will never be the same. Unconditional love has transformed me!"

I went to the concert with my business friend that night. Alice Cooper had no appeal to me. His ridiculous appearance on stage with coffins, bats, and headstones and his garish white and black painted face with fake blood dripping from his mouth was extremely offensive to the Spirit that now dwelled inside of me! I could not wait to get back to my hotel room and away from Alice Cooper. Years later I learned that Alice Cooper became a follower of Jesus Christ.

"Is not my word like a fire? Says the LORD: and like a hammer that [breaks] the rock in pieces?"

Jeremiah 23:29

"And I will give them one heart, and I will put a new spirit within you; and I will take the stony heart out of their flesh, and will give them a heart of flesh."

Ezekiel 11:19

"So, shall my word be that [goes] forth out of my mouth: it shall not return unto me void, but it shall accomplish that which I please, and it shall prosper in the thing [where] I send it."

Isaiah 55:11

"He brought me up also out of a horrible pit, out of the miry clay, and set my feet upon a rock, and established my goings. And he [has] put a new song in my mouth, even praise unto our God: many shall see it, and fear, and shall trust in the Lord."

Psalm 40:2–3

Blessed be the name of the Lord.

Relentless Love

Hot molten metal seeping from my pores.

Fluid iron and copper, silver, bronze, gold.

Rushing river waters cool the melted metals and soothe my burning skin.

They wash the burnished residue away, and the particles rush downstream with the river water. Parts of my soul have gone into the furnace to be fired and purified; others have been carried off by the river water.

Steam wafts from my skin into the air.

Cool rivers flow over me, cleansing and soothing.

Renewing.

I am tugged into the river by the current!

An unseen force pulls my body into the river and drags me to the bottom of the riverbed over smooth river rock; the hardness is pressing indentations into my back and then my front as I am tossed around like a rag doll by the undercurrent, rolling over and over uncontrollably as I remember to breathe, and yet there is no air!

I surface when my legs strike a boulder or a fallen tree.

My face breaks the surface of the water as I gasp for air, my heart beating out of my chest.

I instinctively brush my hands over my arms as if to assist in the removal of the metals that had poured out there, to finish the job.

But there was only smooth skin.

The river water had performed a total cleansing. How simple.

How complex. How warranted. How necessary.

And yet there is that one thing that survived the fiery cleansing: that river rock washing.

Love.

The love survived. Love never fails. Love is never static.

Love cannot be contained. Love survives only to thrive.

Love pursues. To be shared. Unchanging. Relentless. Love.

He pursued me. He won me.

I am His.

I always was...since the foundation of the world.

I am the object of relentless love.

Freedom

I'm leaving something behind.

Can't see it in the rearview mirror. Something weighty and old.

It's time to let go. Time to release regret, loss, grief, grieving loss. Grieving locust eaters.

The plowing was painful and meticulous, thorough and time-consuming.

Time to move on and embrace the wide and wild open road. It's time for my Alaska.

My magic bus.

Time for the eagle to fly. No. Soar.

The air is so easy to breathe at this altitude.

Transvestite in the House

It was a beautiful autumn day, and the sun was shining brightly in Texas. It was lovely, crisp, and still warm outside. The sun was streaming in our center through the sheer, feminine curtains hanging in the windows. I was in our center taking care of last-minute details in our little cottage in the historic district where we operated in Dallas. It was a lovely place that was wooden, painted yellow with white trim, and thoughtfully and tastefully decorated to create a comfortable, warm, and relaxing environment like a home.

It was as far opposite of a cold, institutional abortion facility as you could get. There were plush sofas and comfortable chairs to sit on in the reception and counseling rooms. We had a fully equipped kitchen and dining room, a sonogram room, as well as a meeting room that accommodated additional tables and chairs for presentations and classes. I was preparing for a luncheon to introduce and educate people about our center. The goal was to obtain financial and prayer support for the center, which was completely funded by donors.

As I was flitting about with last-minute details like straightening cushions and arranging flowers and table settings, a visitor opened the large wooden front door. I turned around excitedly, expecting to greet ladies from my church who may have arrived a little early for the event. I was so excited to show them our facility and get to speak to them about our ministry there. Instead, I saw a garish sight. I am sure the shock was apparent on my face, although I tried not to react as I was taught in my counseling education.

There stood a very tall Black man, approximately six foot three, dressed in women's clothing: a blouse, skirt, purse, jewelry, painted fingernails, and garish red lipstick on his giant lips. He literally looked like a basketball player playing dress-up. He had a wig on that was quite long, about mid-back in length. My first thought was, *You've got to be kidding me; my church ladies will be here any minute!* I could not believe I now had this "problem" in the house. I needed to get him out as quickly as possible!

I came to my senses and asked him if I could help him. He replied that he saw our sign from the sidewalk, noting we were a women's center, and wondered how we could help him. I replied that our focus was helping women with unplanned pregnancies, providing free pregnancy tests and counseling as well as other free resource assistance. He laughed rather demurely and said, "Well, I guess you can't really help me then."

He then asked if we had a toilet that he could use. I hesitated for a split-second, thinking about this garish man in our sweet little feminine bathroom, where pregnancy tests were run, decorated especially for the comfort of women, and thought about saying no. I was thinking about the reactions of the church ladies if they were to see this individual when they came in the front door of our quaint little cottage for women.

I said, "Sure. I'll show you where it is." I took him around the corner, and he popped inside. He was inside for a full ten minutes. Every minute that was ticking by, I was imagining how he was defacing our sweet little facility for our beloved clients and how he might be stealing items that would fit into his extra large handbag. I grabbed my cell phone in case the police needed to be called for any reason. I was kicking myself for allowing him to use our facilities.

Finally, he came out. He glanced over at me to see how I might be reacting to his rather protracted stay in the toilet. He headed toward the front door to leave and stopped and grabbed one of my cards in a cardholder on the desk in the reception area. He asked if he could have it to give to any of his friends who might need the type of help that we provided. I said certainly he should do so. I then showed him to the door, and he asked me for directions to a part of the city that I knew, and I gave him walking directions accordingly. I then ran back to see what, if any, havoc he may have wreaked in the toilet and to reclean it in preparation for our lady friends that would arrive any moment.

That's when the Holy Spirit asked me, "What was his name?" I stopped and thought, *I don't know his name.* The Lord rebuked me in my spirit and said, "You don't know his name because you didn't ask him his name. You were, in fact, repulsed by him. I know his name. I created him. He is valuable to me. And I love him as much as I love you or any of your church lady friends who are coming today. From now on, you ask every person who comes through this door their name."

I was so gutted! Convicted in my spirit! How had I been Jesus to this man? All I wanted in the flesh was to get him out of "my" center and clear any evidence of him in preparation for the arrival of the church ladies. I didn't want them "exposed" to this man and his dress and his garish red lipstick. I ran outside and down the front walk of the center, looking down the street to see if I could catch a glimpse of him. I had every intention of yelling out to him if he was still in the area. But he was gone...the opportunity lost.

Jesus loves us all the same...whether church lady, man in woman's clothes with garish red lipstick, post-abortive, stripper, prostitute, office worker, bus driver, rich, or poor.

From that day forward, I never failed to ask anyone who walked in the door of our center his or her name. Jesus was teaching me more than ever to see people as He sees, not as the world sees. I had prayed many, many times for Jesus to allow me to see people through His eyes...and to love those the world deems unlovable like He had loved me.

You Are Known

Psalm 139:1–18 (NIV):

You have searched me, LORD,
and you know me.
You know when I sit and when I rise;
you perceive my thoughts from afar.
You discern my going out and my lying down;
you are familiar with all my ways.
Before a word is on my tongue
you, LORD, know it completely.
You hem me in behind and before,
and you lay your hand upon me.
Such knowledge is too wonderful for me,
too lofty for me to attain.
Where can I go from your Spirit?
Where can I flee from your presence?
If I go up to the heavens, you are there;
if I make my bed in the depths, you are there.
If I rise on the wings of the dawn,
if I settle on the far side of the sea,
even there your hand will guide me,
your right hand will hold me fast.
If I say, "Surely the darkness will hide me
and the light become night around me,"
even the darkness will not be dark to you;

the night will shine like the day,
for darkness is as light to you.
For you created my inmost being;
you knit me together in my mother's womb.
I praise you because I am fearfully and wonderfully made;
your works are wonderful,
I know that full well.
My frame was not hidden from you
when I was made in the secret place,
when I was woven together in the depths of the earth.
Your eyes saw my unformed body;
all the days ordained for me were written in your book
before one of them came to be.
How precious to me are your thoughts, a God!
How vast is the sum of them!
Were I to count them,
they would outnumber the grains of sand—
when I awake, I am still with you.

You are known.

God created you for a purpose.

You are loved by the Holy One.

Since the foundation of the world.

He knows your name.

Undivided Love

YHWH, I am consumed by Your love; it has wrecked me. Burn me up, all of me.

Leave only room for You. I want all of You.

Lord, what do I do with all this passion? "Worship Me."

I am powerless without You; every breath is a gift from You. My heart pants for *You*.

My desire is for all of *You*.

Burn me up, fill me with Your presence, and send me! I raise my hands to You! My heart and my face turn toward You; my eyes are set on Zion.

Give me undivided love.

To serve You until I step from this life into eternity with You.

Thank You for holding me by my right hand and guiding me with Your counsel; thank You for Your transforming love. Oh, great and mighty, Ancient of Days.

Willow: A Desperate Cry

It was Thursday late afternoon, and we were preparing for a staff meeting at our center downtown. The downtown director and I were busily discussing client concerns and things we would bring forward for discussion during our meeting. Soon the time came, and we were all seated around the table in the CEO's office with our drinks and notepads when the receptionist came into the room, quite rattled, and asked for assistance up front with a client. Immediately I jumped up with the downtown director and said we would help. We knew there must be a real need in the waiting room for our staff meeting to be interrupted.

There, seated in the reception area of our downtown facility, sat a noticeably young woman, approximately twenty years old, in a heap of tears, wrecked by emotions. As directors of our facilities, we both sat down and listened to the young woman, trying to decipher her story and assess her needs.

We could ascertain that a Dallas police officer had dropped Willow off at our center. He simply pulled up to the front and pushed her out of his squad car and to our front door that faced a main street downtown. This was highly unusual. Normally, if an officer were bringing a young woman in need to our center, he would stay with her until he greeted us and released her into our care. We understood from Willow's story that she had "met" the officer in a shop downtown, and he had asked if he could give her a ride. He had some free time to spend with her. The directors glanced at each other.

The girl was sobbing hysterically.

Willow weighed only about a hundred pounds. She was very thin and frail. She was of Hispanic ethnicity and was a very pretty, albeit tiny and frail, young woman. She was also very, very troubled. We could piece part of her story together. Finally, I looked directly into her eyes, and I asked her, "Are you a prostitute?" The other director looked at me like I was out of line, but I had heard the Holy Spirit clearly on this, and He prompted me to ask her. At first, she appeared offended that I asked her the question.

Then she started sharing that she had started in the sex industry as a stripper. She had run away from home at an early age due to sexual abuse by an uncle. He had started to molest Willow as an incredibly young child. Eventually, he raped her. When she ultimately broke down and told her mother, she blamed her for the abuse and rape, so she ran away from home. She had no way to support herself, and being homeless, she learned that she could make incredibly good money by stripping.

The stripping had led her to drug use. It was the only way she could force herself to go through with the stripping. The stripping led to more abuse, manipulation, drug use, and eventually, she was coerced into prostituting herself to make more money for herself and her manager, a.k.a. pimp. Indeed, the police officer who had dropped her at our door was a client. He panicked when Willow had a drug-induced breakdown while he was "keeping her company."

She had no place to go but back to her pimp—which she did not want to do. She also had befriended an older man, a fatherly

WILLOW: A DESPERATE CRY

type, who said she could sleep on his sofa. This ultimately led to him inviting her to his bed to "keep warm and cuddle." This ultimately led to a demand for sex as payback for his "support" of her. She did not want to return to this man either.

Every man in Willow's life had used her tiny, fragile body for his own selfish sexual pleasure. Her mother, whether out of the inability to cope with the horror of her own brother raping her child or for some twisted reason inside her (like past abuse), placed the blame on her own child. It seemed that everyone in Willow's life, family or acquaintance, had betrayed her. She was unable to trust anyone. No wonder she turned to drugs to ease the pain.

Suddenly a call came from the staff meeting in the back for us to return to the meeting. We were being pressed to return to the staff meeting. We again gave the leadership an update and began calling around all our shelter contacts to try and find a safe place for Willow to stay. Everyone was already closed for the evening or full. We had no place to take her. There was absolutely no way that we were going to release this vulnerable young woman, now pleading for our help, back on the streets of downtown Dallas that night.

Willow said, "Call Green Oaks. They know me; I can go there." Green Oaks is a reputable facility that assists people in crisis, whether it is a drug, alcohol, emotional, or psychological issue. We called them and gave them Willow's name. They knew her and told us to bring her in. The other director and I advised the rest of the staff that we would not be attending the remainder of the staff meeting—we were leaving to deliver this client to Green Oaks.

When we dropped Willow off at Green Oaks, the staff members who greeted us there were exceedingly kind to her. We were so relieved that she would be in a safe place, at least for a few days, inside their facility, surrounded by kind people who knew her. On the way to the facility, the other director and I shared the Gospel with Willow. She said she had never heard it before and that she had never had people treat her so kindly.

After releasing her into the hands of the professionals at Green Oaks, we went back to our car and prayed for Willow. We prayed for her complete healing—physical, emotional, mental, and spiritual. We prayed that Jesus would reveal Himself to her while she was safely placed inside that facility. We thought about the sovereignty of God and His love for Willow. We thought about how she arrived at our doorstep at just the perfect time that evening. She was not a typical client due to the fact she was not in an "unplanned" pregnancy situation. She was a desperate young woman on the streets of Dallas alone and in desperate need for someone to be Jesus to her.

We were there that night, at the perfect time, to be Jesus to Willow. His timing is perfect; His love is personal. We are called to be His hands and feet on this earth in this life. He calls us to love and be loved. We are called to be Jesus to others in this life.

Immovable

I see the top of a giant tree blowing around forcefully from my fourth-story view.

The natural gentleness of the green leaves in the treetops appears in sharp contrast to the concrete, brick, and steel all around me.

I live next door to a steel mill. Really, right next door. They are not manufacturing molten stuff, but they are manipulating it. I hear the screech of steel bending and cutting beneath the power of mighty tools every day. Shaped into whatever man desires. The steel screeches and moans under the pressure.

But back to the tree. It's a late July day, and it's cloudy in Texas. If you know anything about Texas, you know this is not the norm. The cloud cover is so welcome and embraced, encouraging additional sleep on a day of work should one be so inclined.

Observing the extent to which that enormous treetop is being blown around, at times divided and at times blowing in one direction, I can only ascertain that the wind is blowing hard. I see this from across my loft without my contacts on!

I conclude that the tree must be a very mature one with deeply planted roots, roots in firm ground on a twisted and intense journey for water as its source underground. Above ground the tree seeks sunlight in the sky for nourishment where the branches and limbs have grown upward like lifted arms to embrace the light.

The strong and weathered trunk of the tree was unconcerned with the elements, unmoved by the wind.

Blessed be the name of the Lord.

Fallen Trees, Wayward Satellite Dishes, and Gas Leaks—Spiritual Warfare

I walked up to the center one morning, and a giant pecan tree from our property had fallen into the street, blocking the street, the sidewalk, and the entrance to the neighboring house. I couldn't believe my eyes. For no apparent cause (such as fierce wind or lightning), it had simply fallen in the street. I thought to myself how thankful I was that it had not harmed any people or property. It could easily have fallen on a passing car or pedestrian.

A few days later, I drove up to my own house from the center, and a giant pecan tree fell over the walk up to the front of my house. I could not believe my eyes. It was the same as the fallen tree at the center. No obvious acute cause, no recent wind, storm, or lightning. It just fell.

A couple of weeks afterward, a friend and I were driving up to Oklahoma so she could share her testimony about how Jesus came into her life at my mother's church in Oklahoma. It was a small, little country church. On the drive up, we experienced a huge storm. A storm cloud carrying a tornado was swirling above us. It looked like it might touch down, but it never did. It did, however, blow my car so hard that I decided to pull off the highway and wait for it to pass. It passed on, and the rain let up, and we continued our journey.

As we drove down the winding country road that led to my mother's house in rural Oklahoma, we realized that a giant tree (not sure what kind) had fallen across the roadway. There was absolutely no way the two of us could remove it. We would have to go around.

That meant approximately ten additional miles and approaching from the backside to avoid the fallen tree. I thought, *Lord, what's with the three fallen trees?*

One night as I slept warmly and peacefully in my bed, the phone rang at about 2:30 a.m. I picked it up, and it was the marketing director of our ministry. She told me that the alarm company had called her and advised the alarm was going off at the center where I was director. She said that they should have called me, but they did not have my number and that it was my responsibility to see what was happening. It was likely to be a false alarm. I got dressed and realized that it was indeed storming outside. For some reason, I was compelled to go out to the garage and grab a blue tarp and some duct tape.

When I arrived at the center, I saw what all the fuss was about. The satellite dish had blown off the roof of our sweet little cottage and crashed into a giant plate glass window on the side of the cottage. The glass was everywhere, inside and out. The curtains were blowing out of the window, and it was starting to rain fiercely. I managed to duct tape the tarp over the gaping hole and began looking online for a twenty-four-hour glass company. I learned that night that twenty-four-hour glass companies only answer the phone twenty-four hours. They don't come out until the next morning. So I slept the remainder of that night on the sofa in the center and waited for the glass company to arrive—which they promptly did as promised at 7:30 a.m. I went home and showered and came back with a brand-new window installed and one very banged-up satellite dish hanging from a wire on the side of the cottage.

One afternoon, a sonographer and I were sitting in the dining room of our center discussing clients we had seen that day when all of a sudden, we both became very sleepy.

She confessed that she felt nauseous, and suddenly so did I. She laid her head down on the table. I knew then something was terribly wrong for her to do that. I asked her if she was okay, and she said no.

Just then, a knock came at the front door. I went to the door and greeted a utility worker who advised that they had just hit a gas line on our property. They were doing utility construction on our street. He advised us to get out of the cottage immediately. I ran back to the dining room and grabbed up the sonographer, and we propped open the front door and ran out.

We later learned that after testing, the gas company found five gas leaks under our property. It was a miracle there had not been an explosion or some other potentially terrible incident.

I was beginning to get a full understanding of how the enemy was not happy that we were standing for life and how much He hated those made in the image of God. God was teaching me about spiritual warfare—how to prepare for it, recognize it, and fight it.

Finally, my brethren, be strong in the Lord, and in the power of his might. Put on the whole armour of God, that ye may be able to stand against the wiles of the devil. For we wrestle not against flesh and blood, but against principalities, against powers, against the rulers of the darkness of this world, against spiritual wickedness in high places. Wherefore take unto you the whole armour of God, that ye may be able to withstand in the evil day, and having done all, to stand.

Ephesians 6:10–13

"Fear thou not; for I am with thee: be not dismayed; for I am thy god: I will strengthen thee; yea, I will help thee; yea, I will uphold thee with the right hand of my righteousness" (Isaiah 41:10).

"Be strong and of a good courage, fear not, nor be afraid of them: for the LORD thy God, He is that doth go with thee; he will not fail thee, nor forsake thee" (Deuteronomy 31:6).

Simplicity: Travel Light

Simplicity has been in my heart and my mind for the past three years. When I returned from Bangladesh doing work there with an NGO, I drove up to my 4,000-plus SF home with a three-car garage and a swimming pool close to the lake and became nauseous. I went inside my kitchen and turned on the faucet to get a clean drink of water and marveled at the fact that I could do so and had taken it for granted for my entire life. I had been in a village outside Dhaka where the water was polluted with heavy metals from brick plants upstream. It was unwise to bathe or shower in it; we took baby wipe "baths" to avoid the water as much as possible. Many of the villagers had severe vision problems by age forty because of the poisons in the water. The birth rates were markedly low due to poor nutrition and pollutants.

If you got your hand crushed in an accident, your hand was simply crushed forever. There were no medical services available to "patch you up." We saw a young boy with a deformity of his hand for this very reason; this child would have had a normal hand after receiving medical care in the US.

There were no municipal services there, such as trash pick-up and waste handling. Garbage dumps were mounds of trash on the city street corners that reeked up to high heaven. Even then, the poor would sit on top of them and sift through them, looking for something to eat or worthwhile to keep. The smell of it permeated the air throughout the city, wafting up through the electrical power lines that were strung in a haphazard fashion, twisted, and tied in such a way as to never pass any sort of city code in the United States of America.

My point is that I was wrecked out because of the beautiful people of Bangladesh, who delighted in the simple things in life, such as American candy or having their fingernails painted (even the boys; they were unaware that in America this little luxury was reserved for girls). They lived in tin huts with dirt floors and thatched roofs. Most had no electricity. If they did, it was sporadic and only available a few hours a day. Yet they smiled so readily; they laughed so spontaneously. They didn't walk fast or push people aside in the street. They played with sticks and stalks, and most had no shoes. They wore the same clothes for days. They did not care about hair conditioner because shampoo was such a luxury. We knew this because we brought the villagers a supply, and they did not touch the conditioner. They chose only shampoo.

Jesus wrecked me out on materialism in Bangladesh and began to convict me in the area of simplicity. His message to me was to "simplify" and "travel light." It all started halfway around the world in Bangladesh.

Today I am sitting in Edinburgh, Scotland, writing this post. I have been in Europe since September 24th, starting in London, then venturing to Oxford, and landing in Scotland four days ago. I am marveling at the contrast between the people of Europe and the people of Bangladesh. While Islam dominates Bangladesh, atheism is predominant here. Everyone shares this with us; it's like a badge they wear with pride or simply share matter-of-factly like, "I really have brown hair; this is a color job." One girl shared with us that she would rather be locked in a spooky cemetery than a church. I have found in my own personal experience that most atheists are mad at God for one reason or another. An Englishman said to us unemotionally, "We are a godless people." There are beautiful ancient churches everywhere you look (especially here in Edinburgh), but the light is missing. Churches are empty relics that have become museums, and I couldn't agree more that they are "godless." They are beautiful ancient buildings that reflect man's work but not the love of Christ. Buildings cannot emanate love. Buildings cannot instill truth. Buildings can be idols to humanity's achievements and aspirations and completely devoid of God and his love. These buildings are devoid of any human life except for tourists and caretakers...

Anyway, I digress.

We cannot take any of this "stuff" with us when we leave this planet and this life. I now live in an apartment in a questionable part of downtown Dallas that is less than 700 SF and is inside a 110-year-old former flour mill. My floors are concrete, and my windows are old and leaky. I could not love it anymore! I have great friends and neighbors and tons of freedom because I own fewer things. Truth is, I want to get rid of more things! Truth is, I would sell it all and sublet my apartment to be able to get to Europe and be able to share God's love with the people. They are warm and friendly, authentic, and lovely once you get to know them and get them to open up. Their honesty, however brutal, is refreshing and appreciated. Without knowing Christ personally, they have exhibited more of the character of God than most Christians I know. They have invited us into their homes, fed us, spent time getting to know us, and genuinely valued us as fellow human beings. I have learned volumes from these "godless" people. At one of our destinations, we put out an APB at the local church for a place to stay, and only one person responded to a couple of chicks from America; they would allow us to sleep on their floor. We had a "godless" family invite us in and give us bedrooms and prepare us gourmet meals for three days. We probably had some of our best conversations with this family, and they will never be forgotten.

What is my point? I'm not sure, except to say the message of simplicity and traveling light is not lost on me. There are so many people out there who need to be loved on, and time is ticking!

Miriam: Call 911

It was a beautiful day in the city, and the sun was streaming through the windows of our sweet little cottage. It had been a busy day with back-to-back appointments. The sonographer was present in the center that day, and we were catching up on paperwork before our next client visit, which was scheduled to be the last appointment of the day. The atmosphere in our center was home-like—comfortable and inviting. It was far from clinical and filled with prayer covering and the presence of the Holy Spirit. The lightness and brightness were palpable and a stark contrast to the streets outside.

At about ten minutes until 3:00 p.m., the front door opened, and it was our last scheduled client of the day, arriving a little early as suggested to complete paperwork prior to her appointment. She was a young African American woman, and the moment she entered the center, we could sense her distress. She was clearly scared and extremely nervous, and it was obvious she had been crying. I approached her to greet her and try to put her at ease. She clearly had a baby bump. I was guessing she was twenty to twenty-four weeks pregnant. I asked if I could get her anything to drink and offered her some water or tea—she declined.

As Miriam completed her paperwork, the sonographer and I went into the kitchen and dining area of the house, sat at the table, and began to pray quietly for this young woman. We both sensed that something was terribly wrong and that the young woman was clearly in deep distress. She had come to the center alone. I thought about how, just a few minutes prior, the sonographer and I were marveling at the beautiful day, enjoying the sweetness of the cottage prepared especially for young women like the one now sitting in our reception area in full crisis mode. The absurdity of the mundane struck me as life carried on outside the center.

People sauntered over to the coffee shop next door to purchase their next latte; the construction workers across the street were outside smoking on their work break, and horns were honking up and down McKinney Ave as people rushed around uptown and the downtown areas of Dallas. Inside this place, this cottage, we dealt with matters of life and death every day our doors were open, even on beautiful sunny days like this one. The sweet cottage where we operated was a battleground for life and for the hearts, minds, and souls of people created in the image of God. We signed up for the battle.

Miriam completed her paperwork, and upon review, I called her into our most comfortable counseling room to talk. She suddenly burst into tears and said, "I am going to kill myself." I sat in a chair next to her and leaned in and said, "You have come to the right place today. We are going to help you the best way we know how." She cried extremely hard for about five minutes, and I let her cry and allowed the emotions to flow from her without interruption. Before I had the chance to proceed according to our intake form (which guided us to be able to assess and address needs in a systematic line of questioning), her story began to spill out.

Miriam was twenty years old. Her grandfather had been abusing her since age eight. He impregnated her for the first time at age seventeen, and she delivered his child at age eighteen. She had a two-year-old at home. Her mother did not know it was the grandfather's child. She was pregnant again, and she did not know how she could keep this baby. Her mother knew she was pregnant, believed the pregnancy was due to her daughter "sleeping around," and was threatening to kick her, her unborn child, and her firstborn child out of the house.

Her grandfather lived in the same house. The truth was this young woman had never had sex willingly. She had never had a boyfriend. Her grandfather had threatened to kill Miriam if she ever revealed "their" secret. He threatened to place all the blame on her to deter her from dating young men. This man had psychologically built a cage around this young woman. Miriam again stated that she wanted to die and she was going to kill herself.

I tried to soothe this young woman with words of comfort and encouragement. I grabbed tissues for her to cry into. I gave her water, which she accepted this time. I spoke to her about God being the God of impossible circumstances. I spoke to her about how God ordains all life, even taking into account sin. I spoke to her of the love of Jesus and how He *sees* us and counts all our tears. I told her that was how she had arrived at our center. There are no coincidences in life, only divine appointments. God had ordained the phone call that had led her to our center on this day, at this time, to be received and to be loved—to hear words of comfort extended to her that Jesus would speak, to be offered *truth and hope*.

She looked up at me and said, "I can't go on. I can't go on living. I'm going to kill myself."

I asked her to excuse me for a moment and stepped out and waved the sonographer over. I knew this young woman was in such a state of depression and desperation that she needed more than we could help her with in our center that day. She needed a safe place to stay, where she could receive help and prevent her from harming herself, as her emotional and psychological state was very fragile. I said to the sonographer, "This young woman has just said three times that she is going to kill herself; we have no choice but to call 911."

I turned and walked back into the counseling room and handed her more tissues. I spoke life and love into her as best as I could. I shared the Gospel of Christ with her. I kept telling her how much Jesus loved her, and because He did, He had sent her to us today to get her the help she needed. I told her that additional help was coming and that Jesus would be with her the whole time—that He promised to never leave us or forsake us.

The ambulance arrived, and she lifted her head as she heard it, tears running down her face. "Oh no," she said.

I said, "These people are here to help you too."

I had the sonographer come in and sit with her as I ran outside to speak to the emergency personnel. I pleaded with the head EMT to be very gentle with this girl. I gave him a brief synopsis of her situation. I explained Miriam had said three times that she was going to kill herself, she was pregnant as an act of incest by her grandfather, and that she already had given birth to one child of his, who was now two years old. I told him Miriam had expressed that she was completely hopeless and wanted to die. I asked him to ensure his team would handle her with kindness and empathy. He assured me that they would.

I watched as they prepared to whisk her away to the hospital and noticed that the men of the EMT crew that day were very somber and acting in great kindness toward Miriam.

I prayed silently that she would receive the same treatment once she got to the hospital and that all of the doctors and nurses would treat her with the utmost compassion and dignity. I prayed for Jesus to intervene in a miraculous way in her life.

He reassured me that He just had. As the ambulance pulled away from the center, lights flashing, a small crowd from the coffee shop next door stepped outside with their lattes to see what all the fuss was about next door. The absurdity of the mundane.

Absurdity of the Mundane

(Written in Edinburg, Scotland—October 2013)

I have been pondering the absurdity of the mundane for a long time; this has been a long time coming, but today is certainly the day to write it.

I've often had a tough time processing the absurdity of the mundane. Something certainly most people never think about. As compared to what you might ask. Today was a perfect example.

After a chilly morning shopping excursion in Edinburgh, where Danielle and I were celebrating our shopping deal of the week—an electrical converter that cost one pound at the local equivalent of the dollar store—we were so delighted that we decided to go back to our host Anne's beautiful home and try them out. After all, "it's all about the hair." We laughed.

We plugged in the two new converters and immediately hooked up our necessities—our laptops and iPhones. We sat marveling at how easy they were to use compared to the old one we had broken just this morning and thanked Jesus for our treasured find. We sat down to open our laptops when we heard the screams.

At first, we both froze, thinking possibly children were playing, when we then heard the distinct and desperate cry, "Help me!"

I ran down the stairs and out the front door with Danielle on my heels. We were supposed to be touring the coast, but it was too cold, so we decided to go home and play with our new converters.

We were met by the screams of the next-door neighbor—eyes wide open in terror and her voice hysterical, "My husband has just hanged himself! Help me!"

Danielle ran back into our house for her cell phone. I looked around in desperation as another neighbor drove up. I ran up to her car and basically yanked open her door and asked, "How do you make an emergency call here? Please call for help! This woman's husband has hung himself!"

I ran into the woman's house, and she was coming from the downstairs kitchen with a knife. "What are you doing with that?" I asked. "Give me the knife!"

"No," she said. "I am going to cut him down!" "Is he dead?" I asked.

"Yes," she said, "but I have to cut him down."

I ran up the stairs after her repeating, "Give me the knife!" but she would not listen.

She grabbed an enormous ladder, used by her husband to hang himself from an exceedingly high rafter in the hall closet, and ran up it.

"No!" I screamed.

But it was too late; the rope gave, and his body fell several feet onto the closet floor, crashing into metal electronics stored there and packages of clothing in plastic. I ran over and began to throw off the packages and other items stored in the closet that caved in on him when he fell. Somewhere in the background we were handing off the giant ladder to Danielle, the neighbor who called for emergency assistance, and our hostess, Anne.

He landed on his back in a gruesome thud, completely unconscious. A fleeting thought crossed my mind—if he wasn't dead before, he was surely dead now as hard and awkwardly as he fell. I noticed a terrible gash in his neck.

The woman screamed, "Help me pick him up!" The neighbor said, "Don't move him!"

Emergency was on the phone with her now. All of a sudden, he gasped and groaned and then began seizing.

"He is having a seizure! He has epilepsy!" screamed his wife.

"Let's turn him to his side so he doesn't swallow his tongue," I said. She grabbed his upper body, and I grabbed his legs to turn him.

"No!" said the neighbor. "Don't move him!"

She still had the phone to her ear with the emergency operator on the line. We rolled him back onto his back.

"Leave him on his back and count breaths," the paramedics instructed us.

I watched his chest move and began counting: one, two, three, four, five, six, seven. As I watched his chest move up and down, counting breaths, the Lord clearly impressed me, "This is what I am going to do to my church in the UK; I am going to resurrect it."

I knew the Lord had brought this man back to life. This was not the end of his story. He was clearly alive and breathing and had not swallowed his tongue from the seizure.

A minute later, the ambulance arrived and asked us to move away from the closet.

"You saved his life," I said to his wife, and I hugged her until tears rolled down her cheeks.

"Do you have family in the city?" I asked. "Yes, I have three children in school."

"Do you have anyone else that you want us to call for you?" I asked. "No."

"Do you have a sister, or is your mother here in Edinburgh?" I asked. "No, just his family," she replied, "my in-laws."

The paramedics took over and began working on him calmly and confidently. Later I asked them why they did not immediately put him on oxygen, and they explained that they had checked his oxygen level immediately and found him to be oxygenating properly at 97 percent.

The police arrived and asked us all to go downstairs so they could sort things out.

I stayed with her downstairs, patting her and putting my arm around her. I kept reassuring her that she had saved his life by cutting him down and that was a good thing.

The family was Sikh and had suffered financially due to his epilepsy. He was unable to drive. He had recently lost his driver's license because he had crashed into several cars after having a seizure. He would not be able to continue to work as a taxi driver.

Arrangements were made for the two younger children about to be released from school. In the meantime, the seventeen-year-old son arrived home from school and was clearly shaken.

"Why are the police here?" he kept asking.

The ambulance took off with the man's wife in the back seat and the son in the passenger seat. We were praying the whole time.

When the man initially became semiconscious, he was angry and hit the floor with his fists. He was telling us to leave him alone using expletives.

We prayed that Jesus would reveal Himself to this man personally in a dramatic way and that He would also reveal Himself to his wife and comfort her. We prayed for comfort and healing for the son and that he would in no way assume responsibility or take on guilt for the act of his father.

Meanwhile, people on the streets carried on discussing the wintry weather, shivering at the stiff winds, and scurrying to their own destinations. The neighbors discussed the numerous qualities they disliked about the family and how awkward it felt to interact with them in such a time of crisis.

Her name was Ravi, and all I could really do for her was give her a hug. I know without a doubt in my mind that is the reason God ordained our every step today. That is why we heard her screams for help. His timing is perfect.

We came all the way from the United States of America to London, to Oxford, and then to Edinburgh just for Ravi today. I am reassured of God's goodness in that He would orchestrate all of that for Ravi.

His lovingkindness reaches up to the sky.

Anayah: God Answers Misdirected Call

I was working late in the center one evening like I often did to catch up on paperwork and reports. The amount of paperwork and reporting for a non-profit operation like ours was extraordinary. This was not my favorite part of my calling. I was one hundred percent at this center for the women. I also knew if we could reach the heart of the women through the love and compassion of Jesus, more than one life would be saved.

When the Lord called me into the pregnancy center ministry, He also gifted me with an amazing, unconditional love and compassion for the women. Jesus loved them through me. This love could only flow from Him. Sometimes my director friend in the downtown center called me the "love lady." She would send her most challenging clients to me for counseling. I prayed for years at my kitchen table for God to help me to love the unlovable like He had loved me. I prayed that He would break my heart for what broke His. I prayed that He would help me to see people through the eyes of Jesus. God answered my prayers. He equips us for what He calls us to do.

Years later, when working in ministry in England, I complained to the Lord, "Why do You have me here with these people, Lord? They are so hard! They are so rude! They are extremely unlovable!" (Those who seemed to be the hardest were professing Christians!) I felt like Jonah and the Assyrians! He didn't let me dwell in that place for one minute. He spoke, "You asked Me to teach you to love the unlovable."

After all, Jesus said to *love*. We are not to apply our own idea of worthiness as a condition for love. The people who act the least lovely are the ones crying out the loudest for love, something they may likely have never experienced.

At about 6:30 p.m., the phone rang. I normally would let a call at this hour go to voicemail and then check it to see if it were urgent. I did not like interruptions from sales calls. But this call came in via a service our center subscribed to that directed calls for pregnancy help to our center, so I answered it. On the other end of the line was a very distraught young woman named Anayah.

She was pregnant and had just been severely beaten. It was not the first time Anayah had been beaten during her pregnancy. Her husband was a Muslim, she said. He beat her for senseless reasons. She was crying hysterically and needed someone to talk to and needed a safe place to go. He had pushed her down the stairs this time, and she was very worried about her safety and the health of the baby. She wanted to get away from him, but she was afraid to leave.

I spoke to Anayah on the phone for approximately forty minutes, trying to calm her, reassure her, and build a rapport with her so that she would have a level of trust that would allow her to come in and visit face to face. When we finally got to that point, I asked her to come in and speak with me. I started giving her details on our location. It was at this point that both of our hearts sank like a stone upon the realization that Anayah was calling from Florida and had somehow been directed to our center in Dallas, Texas.

She started wailing and crying again. Just when it looked like we had given her an inkling of hope and assured her that there were people out there who cared about her situation and were prepared to help her with all the resources available to them, we now had a huge problem—our center was located halfway across the country in Dallas. However, I reassured her that there were centers just like ours in her area and people who worked there that cared just like the people in our center, that pregnancy help centers exist to help people just like her.

After taking Anayah's phone number and reassuring her I would phone back, I hung up and began searching for centers near her through a pregnancy help partnership organization our ministry belonged to. I was able to refer her to a center in Florida where she was able to go and receive help for her many needs. I was so thankful for all the organizations that worked together to make these connections and resources available to people nationally.

One late afternoon many weeks later, after a terrible week and all the staff and volunteers had left the center, I laid my head on my desk and cried. I just poured out my heart to the Lord. I was so broken over the condition of our culture and the condition of the church that was not impacting our culture. As a result, professing Christians were coming into our center actually contemplating abortion as an "option" for their unplanned pregnancy.

I mourned over the fact that we now had clear scientific evidence to show these young women that life begins at conception; we could allow them to listen to the baby's heartbeat and actually see the baby via sonogram, and yet abortion was still considered an "option" for women—even those claiming to be Christian. I poured out my heart and frustration to the Lord. I asked Him, "Lord, why do You have me here? What difference are we making? What can I do? This problem is too big for me! It's too hard!"

After I had myself a good cry, the Lord disallowed me to feel sorry for myself by reassuring me that no problem was too big for Him:

"Behold, I am the LORD, the God of all flesh: is there anything too hard for me?"

Jeremiah 32:27

I was to be faithful and obedient and leave the consequences to Him. *My job was to love, and His business was to transform lives.* My pity party was over, and I opened up my computer to clean up my email. I found a remarkably interesting email in my spam that evening.

The email had been sitting in my spam for two months. It had been a while since I had checked my spam folder. It was a message from Anayah! She thanked me for saving her and her baby's life. She had gone into early labor a few days after our phone call that evening due to the abuse by her husband. Her baby had been born prematurely, had stayed in the hospital for several weeks, and had just been released to go home. She reported that the baby was doing well now and thriving.

Prior to her early labor, she had been able to connect with the pregnancy help center in Florida, where she lived. They were able to help her with many of her needs in addition to providing her with assistance to get to a safe place to live. She no longer had to fear abuse at the hands of her husband. She no longer had to fear for the life of her child. Anayah had given birth to a beautiful baby boy, and she sent me a picture.

Loving and serving these women has been the biggest privilege of my life. The call I answered that evening after hours came into our center exactly as it was supposed to. All I had to do was answer the call.

His love never fails.

> *If I speak in the tongues of men or of angels, but do not have love, I am only a resounding gong or a clanging cymbal. If I have the gift of prophecy and can fathom all mysteries and all knowledge, and if I have a faith that can move mountains but do not have love, I am nothing. If I give all I possess to the poor and give over my body to hardship that I may boast, but do not have love, I gain nothing.*
>
> *Love is patient, love is kind. It does not envy, it does not boast, it is not proud. It does not dishonor others, it is not self-seeking, it is not easily angered, it keeps no record of wrongs. Love does not delight in evil but rejoices with the truth. It always protects, always trusts, always hopes, always perseveres.*
>
> *Love never fails. But where there are prophecies, they will cease; where there are tongues, they will be stilled; where there is knowledge it will pass away. For we know in part, and we prophesy in part, but when completeness comes, what is in part disappears. When I was a child, I talked like a child, I reasoned like a child. When I became a man, I*

put the ways of childhood behind me. For now, we see only a reflection as in a mirror; then we shall see face to face. Now I know in part; then I shall know fully, even as I am fully known.

And now these three remain; faith, hope and love. But the greatest of these is love.

1 Corinthians 13 (NIV)

Your Love Is Enough

All my life I have sought to be loved, to be valued, treasured. Abandoned and ignored, I felt rejected, invisible, unworthy of love.

I sought to fulfill the need for human love elsewhere, the need to be special to someone, the need to be loved unconditionally.

The need to be validated.

Wrong relationships never mended the brokenness of my heart and never filled the God-sized hole in it; they only produced and reproduced the feelings of abandonment, rejection, and unworthiness.

After I became a follower of Christ in 2003 after encountering Him in a hotel room in Tulsa, Oklahoma, my life changed.

After He showed me that I was a sinner, Christ lovingly wrapped His arms around me and poured His love out over me.

It permeated every fiber of my being as He enveloped me in His beautiful presence. I would never be the same.

For the first time in my life, I experienced unconditional love.

A priceless gift freely given—nothing I had earned or deserved.

Nothing I could ever do would separate me from it. I was done.

I was undone.

Never to be the same.

Later, He gifted me with a love for the unlovable. There were many hard lessons while developing this gift.

Many times, I asked, "Lord, why?" His reply was always the same, "I am teaching you to love the unlovable like I loved you before you were clothed in the robes of My righteousness." Wow.

So last night I was touched by love in the shape of a heart in a baked sweet potato—really. Feeling lonely and a little sorry for myself, I looked down at the sweet potato I had just cut open to butter, and the two halves had split into the shape of a perfect heart.

I sensed God's presence in my little kitchen and heard Him whisper His love in my ear. That is a personal God.

That is a loving Savior.

That is a love you can count on. That is unconditional love.

Your love is enough.

"I will sing unto the LORD as long as I live: I will sing praise to my God while I have my being. My meditation of him shall be sweet: I will be glad in the LORD."

Psalm 104:33–34

A Message in Bottles

It was May of 2013, and I was driving down Mockingbird Lane in Dallas, Texas, to get my car inspected. I was listening to some music in my bright yellow (a.k.a. "Sunburst," the color officially given by Toyota) FJ Cruiser, thinking about absolutely nothing, when I had an open vision. The song on the radio that was playing was by Sting and called "Message in a Bottle."

It was the first time in my life I had an open vision. It was of a beach with beautiful blue waves rolling in on the shore. The gentle waves were carrying millions of bottles that appeared to be unbelievably valuable, jewel-like, and they were washing up onto the shore. The bottles were fairly small translucent glass of various shapes but all similarly sized, and the sun was shining through each one as it rolled onto the sand. Each bottle was "outlined" in an iridescent color—all the assorted colors of the rainbow. I knew in my spirit that these bottles were valuable; each one was unique in shape and color. The colors of the waves were various shades of blue—from a beautiful deep cobalt blue to a turquoise Caribbean color of blue. As the bottles washed up and landed on the shore, they sparkled with light and brilliant color. I looked down at the beach and marveled at the fact that the bottles were stretched out for miles—as far down the beach as I could see—they were piled up! There appeared to be millions and millions of them washing up on shore and stacking up miles and miles down the beach. There were stacks and stacks of them piled high.

I noted that inside each bottle was what looked like a little "pod." That was the first word that came to my mind. Somehow, I knew that the "pods" contained in the bottles were precious.

It was almost seed-like in shape, about the size of an avocado or prune seed. I did not know what it was, so I asked, "Lord, what are those pods inside these beautiful bottles?"

His answer was immediate:

"These are the aborted babies that the world has forgotten and discarded like trash, but each one is a precious jewel to me."

My spirit was rocked! I was so grieved as God was showing me *His heart* for the aborted and discarded children through this vision on the beach—this image of jeweled beauty, the way He sees these babies. I wept in my car. I wept for God's heart on the matter. I wept for all the babies discarded like garbage. I wept at the overwhelming vastness of the castaways—piled up too innumerable to count. I wept for all the babies God valued like precious jewels, His creative handiwork discarded like rubbish by the world.

I wept for all the women who had been wounded by abortion. I wept for all the bloodlines that had ended with those babies. I wept for all the *loss.* I wept for lost potential. I wept for humanity. I wept that truth has fallen to the ground on the streets of America. I wept for all those denied life! But mostly I wept because the Father had shown me *His heart and His grief* over the matter. He has not forgotten. He sees. He is heartbroken.

While in New Zealand in the fall of 2015, I was thinking one day about God's Word and how precious it is. I was thanking God for His

Word and was trying to think of a word, an item of proper value that would describe and capture how precious it is, and the most accurate description I could think of was "jewel." I said, "Lord, I love Your Word! Your Word is like a precious jewel!"

The Lord immediately brought to my mind the vision of the bottles that I had in 2013. He said, "Those jewels in the bottles also represent my Word. My precious Word has been aborted and discarded by the world like the babies." I cried out in grief; I felt gutted. I was literally weeping for God's heart. I was weeping for the utter disregard of our societies that ignore and discard the most valuable things imaginable. The most precious thing, His Word, and His creation—babies made in His image. We are rejecting the precious seed of life. My soul grieved at the implications. My soul grieved for the Father's heart on the matter.

The Lord impressed upon me this parallel: the unwanted child being endangered in the one place in the world it should be the safest, its mother's womb, and the Word of God being "aborted" (torn apart) and cast out of the church—the place where His Word, the Bible, should be safest. His words are being ignored, taken out of context, diminished, or taken apart "limb by limb" in many churches that claim His name.

While still working at the pregnancy center as a staff member in 2013, after an exceedingly difficult day and client appointments, I laid my head down on my desk and cried out to the Lord in great sorrow and grief as to why the church was not impacting the culture. Why were women professing to be Christians coming in our center and inquiring about abortion? There was a church on almost every corner in Dallas, Texas! Why was the church not impacting the culture? Why was the culture impacting the church?

God answered me, "Because they are watering down my Gospel."

There is a much-overlooked story in the book of Jeremiah. In chapter 36 the king of Judah, Jehoiakim, receives a message from Jeremiah from God written in a scroll. The king had the scroll read aloud in front of all the princes that stood beside him. The king did not like the message that the scroll contained—the very words of God to the king of Judah. So he cut up the scroll with a knife and cast it into the fire that was on the hearth.

Ezekiel 16:20–21 says:

> *Moreover, [you have] taken [your] sons and [your] daughters, whom [you have] borne [to] me, and [have] sacrificed unto them to be devoured. Is this of [your] whoredoms a small matter? That [you have] slain my children, and delivered them to cause them to pass through the fire for them?*

Israel lost her nation as a punishment for the sin of idolatry that manifested in many forms. The root cause of this idolatry was casting out or ignoring the Word of God, which ultimately led to the sacrifice of baby sons and daughters created in the image of God to the God of Moloch. *The rejection of the Word of God is the rejection of life. God's Word and life are synonymous.*

> *In the beginning was the Word, and the Word was with God, and the Word was God. The same was in the begin-*

ning with God.

All things were made by him; and without him was not anything made that was made.

In him was life; and the life was the light of men.

John 1:1–4

In return for ashes, God is going to give beauty. The ashes of the Word of God thrown into the fire, the ashes of the babies being burned in the fires of Moloch, the ashes of the aborted babies whose bodies are incinerated like "medical waste"—all beautiful jewels and seeds of flowers for Zion—the beautiful jewels that are the foundation of New Jerusalem, living stones, sparkling jewels. God has not forgotten; God will redeem; He is righteous.

"For if the casting away of them be the reconciling of the world, what shall the receiving of them be, but life from the dead?" (Romans 11:15).

"For the Lord shall comfort Zion: he will comfort all her waste places; and he will make her wilderness like Eden, and her desert like the garden of the Lord; joy and gladness shall be found therein, thanksgiving, and the voice of melody" (Isaiah 51:3).

> *The Spirit of the Lord God is upon me; because the Lord [has] anointed me to preach good tidings to the meek; he [has] sent me to bind up the brokenhearted, to proclaim liberty to the captives, and the opening of the prison to them are bound;*
>
> *To proclaim the acceptable year of the Lord, and the day of vengeance of our God; to comfort all that mourn;*

To appoint unto them that mourn in Zion, to give to them beauty for ashes, the oil of joy for mourning, the garment of praise for the spirit of heaviness; that they might be called trees of righteousness, the planting of the Lord, that he might be glorified.

Isaiah 61:1–3

"For Zion's sake I will not hold my peace, and for Jerusalem's sake I will not rest, until the righteousness thereof goes forth as brightness, and the salvation thereof as a lamp that [burns]" (Isaiah 62:1).

"Thus [says] the Lord of hosts; I am jealous for Jerusalem and for Zion with a great jealousy" (Zechariah 1:14).

"I bring near my righteousness; it shall not be far off, and my salvation shall not tarry: and I will place salvation in Zion for Israel my glory" (Isaiah 46:13).

Sailing with the Anchor

I'm setting sail with the anchor of my soul across the North Atlantic, where the cold winds blow. Perched in the crow's nest where the view is best, listening to my heart beating out of my chest.

I'm setting sail with the anchor of my soul.

I'm setting sail where the cold winds blow.

Who ever knew I'd be steered right toward that cold North Sea?

Only one thing's for sure—that you are here with me. I'm setting sail with the lover of my soul.

Sails wide open as the mighty wind blows.

Fear escapes me as I am tossed back and forth 'cause I'm setting sail.

With the anchor of my soul. The canvas sails are full, billowing from those cold north winds.

The seas roll black as my hair blows back. The salt spray stings as my eyes become slits.

But I can see fine with them shut tight from the brine.

'Cause I'm not steering.

This seaworthy vessel.

I'm not the captain with the stripes and the plans; I'm just a passenger who said yes to the journey. Never looking back, pressing on toward the prize.

Face turned toward Zion.

As the waves grow larger, there's a fire that's gone before me, burning on the other side.

Water surrounds me on this journey.

On this wild sea ride.

I smile as I press in toward the captain of my soul. This ship is such a lovely vessel.

Piloted by the anchor of my soul. Warmed by the fire within as I'm tossed to and fro.

Onward against the wind as the north wind blows.

Flowers for Zion: Redemption

It was May 2015, and I was staying on a ranch in England right outside Oxford. I had been in England for about three months. While at the ranch, a young woman had given me an exceptionally large canvas to paint on. I offered to pay her for it, but she gave it to me because it had a small imperfection on one corner of it, and it was a thin, cheap type of stretched canvas as well—a practice canvas, not one on which to paint a serious painting.

I had not been able to paint in over six months, and certainly not since I had arrived in England. I made my way into Oxford and purchased some reasonably priced acrylic paints and brushes at the local Hobbycraft store. I could not wait to get back to the ranch and get started. A painting was burning inside me, and it was time to get it out on canvas.

When I returned to the ranch, I quickly set up my painting area inside my room there, and the paint began to flow and land on the canvas out of a deep place inside me like never before. I was not thinking at all about what I was painting. I was simply allowing the brush to dip into the paint and flow out of the brush, guided gingerly by my hand onto the canvas from my spirit.

It was a large canvas—approximately thirty-two by forty-six inches—and I was surprised when I finished that I had only been painting for one hour. The entire painting had gushed forth and was finished in one hour! I stood back and looked at the painting. I noticed two things about it.

It mysteriously looked remarkably similar to a painting I had painted about twelve years earlier, and I had used a color scheme I wouldn't ordinarily choose. It was bright pinks, purples, and blues, along with many other colors under the rainbow. I thought it rather odd that it looked so similar to a painting I painted so many years ago, especially since I was giving it no thought whatsoever and just allowed the paint to flow via the dance of the brush.

Later that evening, my friend came in and spotted the painting, which I had already hung up on the wall beside my bed. She asked me what it was. I said I didn't really know, but it flowed out of a place from deep within my spirit. I told her how I had managed to paint the entire painting in only an hour. She couldn't believe it! She commented on the colors, purple being one of her favorites. As she started to walk out the door, she turned and said, "Hey, you know, that looks like a fetus—a baby in utero." I stared at the painting, and it struck me; it absolutely did look like a baby in utero.

Later, after I had spent time reading my Bible and in prayer, I looked up at the picture. It already held a special place of value for me—I knew that picture had come directly out of my spirit. I said, "Lord, what is that? Why am I painting paintings that are similar? What is this painting about?"

I immediately sensed the presence of the Holy Spirit in the room. He answered me, "You are giving flowers to your baby, Zion. You are honoring him."

Wow. Tears stung my eyes, and it felt like an arrow pierced my heart. Years earlier the Lord had revealed to me that my baby that

I had aborted at age fifteen was a boy. As part of a post-abortion healing program that suggested naming your baby as part of the healing process, I had named my baby Zion. I was honoring my child; I was calling him to remembrance in spirit and honoring him, memorializing him with flowers. The painting contained flowers and butterflies that sprung up before the baby image like a gift being offered.

Then the Lord said, "The way you love this baby is the way I love Zion—with immeasurable love."

I understood the Lord was speaking of layers of meanings: my baby Zion and all the aborted babies discarded by the world as rubbish, each one like a precious jewel to Him; His "child" Zion; His people; His land; His jewels. Once rejected and abandoned— now recognized, affirmed, and *honored in love*. I had such peace and love in my heart. God's *immeasurable love* poured out and over me. I knew that one day, everything, *everything*, was going to be redeemed. God was making everything brand new.

Love Song

The Lord is my refuge, my rock, my redeemer, my strength, my song, my hope, and my joy.

He holds me by my right hand; He guides me with His counsel. His mercies are unending; His joy comes in the morning.

I am thankful! I thank You for my life, its purpose, Your love, joy, peace that passes understanding, hope, contentment in Your abundant provision, friends, brothers and sisters in Christ, Your Holy Spirit, the Spirit's fire, Your calling, that Your thoughts are higher than my thoughts, and Your ways, which are higher than my ways. Thank You for divine appointments and connections. I am in awe of You.

I stand in wonder of You.

Overwhelmed by the power of Your presence.

I can't wait to see what You are going to do!

Lord, You know the desire of my heart; I know You will give me that desire when I am ready. Thank You for the preparation that is already taking place.

I thank You for Your mercy, which manifests as patience and tender loving-kindness toward me.

I thank You for Your unending, immeasurable love.

I thank You for pouring it out over me in rivers of water. Cascading down over my head in rivulets down my body. I thank You for the healing properties contained therein.

I thank You that it is so pure, lovely, holy, and infinite that I cannot truly comprehend it. There is no other God like You! You are the One true God!

You are a God that loves.

You are the definition of love.

I love that my thoughts cannot capture You, that my spirit cannot contain You.

That Your nature is divine, and Your presence is gentle yet powerful and overwhelming.

I love to sense the power of Your presence that makes my head bow in awe and reverence. And yet You gently persuade me to lift up my head and encounter You in love.

My heart sings for You. My spirit aches for You. My mind dwells on You.

My flesh desires to be enveloped in Your presence. Pour my life out like a drink offering.

Not as payback.

But because of my thankfulness to You. YHWH.

The Bridegroom

Jesus, You are beautiful! My bridegroom!

Your eyes are like fire! Your love is pure, Your fragrance lovely, Your countenance brighter than the sun, and You are altogether holy.

Your robe is white and dipped in blood; Your robes clothe me in righteousness. I love You! I am Yours, and You are mine.

"Follow Me." "I will!"

"Do you trust Me?" "Yes!"

"Do you trust Me?" "Yes!"

"Do you trust Me?" "I do!"

"Rest in Me.

"Dwell in My presence.

"Walk with Me.

"Hold My hand. I will never leave you or forsake you. LeAnn."

"Yes?"

"I love you."

Ganei Chaim: Garden of Life

In the fall of 2013, as I was gazing out my fourth-story window, crying out to the Lord about my broken heart, the Lord did something mysterious. He showed me a vision of my heart. As I lay on my bed crying out from my very heart to God while looking out my floor-to-ceiling windows at a beautiful full moon, He gave me a picture of myself lying on the bed.

In that picture I lay weeping tears of blood in despair due to the sorrow in my soul. Then He showed me a picture of my heart. It was alive and beating, red and full of oxygen. My heart was entangled by green vines that were squeezing it. I remember two thoughts that flashed through my mind. The first was, *I am still alive, and my heart is alive and beating.* The second thought was, *At least the vines that are entangling my heart are green and alive.*

As I lay pondering the condition of my heart, it was as if the Lord took a giant pair of scissors and snipped off the places that were being squeezed. The vine was still circling my heart, but my heart was no longer fighting the vine. I could breathe! My heart had been rescued! My heart was set free! The Lord had given me the gift of an unbound heart.

It was now May of 2017, and I stood in a beautiful garden in Latrun, Israel, approximately twenty minutes outside Jerusalem. I was there with a group to plant trees in Ganei Chaim (the "Garden of Life") in memory of children lost to abortion or miscarriage. I was there with Sandi, the director of Bead Chaim Pregnancy Center in Jerusalem, Israel. I had met Sandi at a fundraising event for her ministry in 2013 in Dallas. The same year that God had given me the vision of my heart.

Monks who owned the land had donated the garden to Sandi. They had given her approximately five acres for a garden with the specific purpose of memorializing these precious unborn babies. The view was beautiful. The garden was situated on a small hillside that led down to a small lake. The Judean mountains lined the horizon across the valley. I thought to myself, *Lord, let Zion be close to the water.* I wanted to plant my tree in memory of Zion, facing the water. As we approached, the gardener ran up and told Sandi and the group of a recent fire started by teens in the garden. They were spending time together in the garden one night the previous week and started a campfire that got out of control. The fire ended up burning a large section of the garden down by the water. I thought to myself, *You are kidding me—beauty for ashes.* I knew what was about to unfold, and I smiled to myself because God is just like that.

The gardener led us down the path where he had pre-dug holes for the trees to be planted due to the extreme hardness of the land. Guess where the gardener dug the holes? Right in the middle of the burned tree remains and the ashes, down by the lake, facing the water.

I walked with my tree and chose a spot in the middle of those gray ashes and near a burned-out tree that had a lovely curved shape to it. Beauty for ashes. The great exchange. I knelt and placed that cypress tree into the soil of the land of Israel, and I lovingly scooped up the dirt and the ashes and placed them around the root of the tree.

There was a small boulder a couple of feet away from the tree that would help me mark the exact tree in the future. Some around me fussed over the location due to the ashes and the remaining burned-up trees. I smiled to myself, thinking how *sovereign* my God is. Yes, Zion would be memorialized there. Beauty was breaking forth from the ashes for all to see. In that moment, I recalled the unbound heart vision where God had rescued me by performing a work that only He could do on my heart. I thought about His work of redemption and restoration in my heart. I thought about how life comes full circle. I felt my heart soar over those Judean hills as I reveled in the goodness of the Lord.

The Lord's love for me in that place, that garden, was tangible. I reveled in His love. It was as if time had stopped and everything was moving in slow motion. I sensed His love for all and His desire to redeem and restore everything. I sensed His love for Zion—Zion, my child, Zion, His child. The Lord loves. The Lord redeems. The Lord restores. I pictured beautiful wildflowers popping up all over Zion as the keeper of the gate of the garden of life continued his mission of bringing forth beauty out of ashes.

Blessed be the name of the Lord.

Isaiah 61:11:

"For as the earth [brings] forth her bud, and as the garden [causes] things that are sown into it to spring forth; so, the LORD God will cause the righteousness and praise to spring forth before all the nations."

Bereshit (Genesis): Mathematics of Eternity
The Universe Must Have Had a Beginning According to Cosmologists

"In the beginning was the Word, and the Word was with God, and the Word was God" (John 1:1).

The Lord has taught me over the years that physical condition is often a manifestation of spiritual condition. The truth is that, as Christians, we are in a battle. When we become Christ followers by responding to His *immeasurable love* for us, our spiritual lives are transformed by His grace. We no longer live for the world but for the kingdom of God. We also have entered into a spiritual battle. You can expect that He will train you for the battle and for (His) glory. You will be loved and hated, and you will be both blessed and crucified (Luke 6). Jesus' life reflected simplicity, strength, and sacrifice. He was hated for delivering penetrating truth and for taking a stance that was a radical departure from social norms. Jesus was countercultural. He was and is radical. He requires radical abandonment of our own lives to become His disciple.

"The student is not above the teacher, but everyone who is fully trained will be like their teacher" (Luke 6:40, NIV).

Let's take a look at Jesus' life. From what we know from the Bible, His life was not characteristic of comfort, convenience, exemption from pain, and relative morality. As Christ followers, should we expect to live a different life than the one Christ lived? Jesus lived a sinless life. The Bible tells us we are sinners from birth. A life typical of Western values is exactly the opposite of Christ's; the goal and the expectation is a life of happiness, comfort, prosperity, pain-free living, sacrifice-free, and relative morality. We desire the good things, the advantages of the cross, of following Christ, but not the part that Jesus Himself talks about: sacrifice, dying to self, putting others first, dying to materialism, or living for kingdom (eternal) values versus worldly (passing away) values.

Christ, the bridegroom, is coming very soon for His inheritance: His people and His land. All of His people from every nation, kindred, and tongue (language) will be gifted to Him as His bride. His kingdom will be set up on earth, and He will rule from Jerusalem. All nations will bow down and worship before Him at His throne. He is the King of kings and worthy of worship.

Jesus was born into the world to bear witness to the truth. Jesus Himself answers the question of why He was born, *"To this end was I born, and for this cause came I into the world, that I should bear witness unto the truth. Every one that is of the truth [hears] my voice"* (John 18:37).

Jesus said in John 14:6, *"I am the way, the truth, and the life: no man [comes] unto the Father, but by me."* In this statement, He claims to be our all in all—our way, our truth, and our life. Truth is a person, and it is Jesus Christ.

Jesus also said in John 8:12, *"I am the light of the world: he that [follows] me shall not walk in darkness, but shall have the light of life."*

Jesus tells us He is the *light*, the *way*, the *truth*, and the *life*. The light illumes truth, and the light illumes the way, and it all equals *life*.

Jesus equals life! How beautiful!

> *Whosoever [believes] that Jesus is the Christ is born of God:*
> *and everyone that [loves the father loves his child as well.*
> *This is how] we know that we love the children of God: [by*
> *loving] God and [keeping] his commandments. [In fact,]*
> *this is love for God: [to keep his commands.] And his com-*
> *mands are not [burdensome], for [everyone] born of God*
> *[overcomes] the world. This is the victory that [has over-*
> *come] the world, even our faith.*
>
> *Who is it that [overcomes] the world? [Only the one who*
> *believes] that Jesus is the Son of God.*

1 John 5:1–5

Jesus was born into the world in the form of a man. He, being fully God and fully man, lived a sinless life as a man, and in obedience to His father's will, died a criminal's death on a cross to become the sacrifice for the sin of all humanity and for all time. He was the perfect blood sacrifice required for the propitiation of sin. He was the great exchange, the great sacrifice: His life for all mankind so that man could be reconciled to God the Father. His desire is that none should perish.

"For God so loved the world that he gave his only begotten Son, that whosoever believeth in him should not perish, but have everlasting life" (John 3:16).

But the cross was not the end of the story. On the third day, Jesus was resurrected in glory, and He lives eternally seated at the right hand of the Father. This is our blessed hope! Jesus is alive! His desire is to fellowship with you. If you have never submitted to the lordship of Jesus Christ in your life, I pray you will do so today. He stands and knocks at the door. He's waiting for you to open it.

Jesus said, *"If [you] continue in my word, then [you are] my disciples indeed; and [you] shall know the truth, and the truth shall make you free"* (John 8:31–32).

Read John chapter 10 as Christ describes Himself as the good shepherd that gives life to His sheep. Get into the Word of God and seek fellowship with other Christ followers who are sitting under sound biblical teaching. The way to be sure of sound teaching is to read the Bible for yourself and know what it says. Then you will recognize truth from error. Seeds of truth with a mixture of man's conclusive ideas are not truth. Jesus tells us He is the measure. He is the truth.

My hope and prayer are that you will eagerly await this day.

After this I beheld, and lo, a great multitude, which no man could number, of all nations, and kindreds, and people, and tongues, stood before the throne, and before the Lamb, clothed with white robes, and palms in their hands.

And cried with a loud voice, saying, Salvation to our God which [sits] upon the throne, and unto the Lamb.

And the angels stood round about the throne, and about the elders and the four beasts, and fell before the throne on their faces, and worshiped God.

Saying, Amen: Blessing, and glory, and wisdom, and thanksgiving, and honor, and power, and might be unto our

God forever and ever. Amen.

Revelation 7:9–12

The beauty of God's Word is enduring—it remains and stands forever. Jesus is the Word of God.

This is my prayer:

Lord, let me pour out the tears I've cried and You've collected in that fragrance-filled alabaster jar onto Your beautiful nail-scarred feet and wipe them with my hair. This is our love story, a story of immeasurable love.

Let me be known as a servant of the Lord.

Isaiah 62:4 (NIV):

"No longer will they call you Deserted or name your land Desolate. But you will be called Hephzibah[1] and your land Beulah[2] for the LORD will take delight in you, and your land will be married."

Isaiah 62:11–12:

> *Behold, the LORD [has] proclaimed unto the end of the world, say [you] to the daughter of*
>
> *Zion, Behold, [your salvation comes]; behold his reward is with him, and his work before him.*
>
> *And they shall call them, the holy people, the redeemed of the LORD: and [you shall] be called, Sought out, A city not forsaken.*

Epilogue

Since the writing of this book, there have been new attitudes emanating from women who have had abortions. Due to the cultural pressure to accept abortion as a "health care option," more and more women are publicly "celebrating" their abortions. Celebrities are publicly acknowledging and celebrating by telling their own abortion stories. They speak publicly and wear pins with the date and sometimes location of the clinic where they received their abortion.

In this country, we now have satanists who are opening their own abortion clinics, admitting they use the aborted babies in "religious rituals."

I can honestly say in my eight years of experience, encountering hundreds, maybe thousands of women and girls, I never ever encountered anything but grief, loss, and regret when counseling post-abortive women.

These new attitudes are a chilling reflection of the manifestation of evil, manifested in pride, and promoted and propagated by a culture that has asked God to "stay out" of society.

Spiritually, abortion is modern-day child sacrifice. It is nefariously promoted as a human right. The devil has always been a liar and deceiver. It is modern-day sacrifice to the pagan gods of the Old Testament, manifesting in modern times.

Ezekiel 16:20–21:

Moreover, [you have] taken [your] sons and...daughters, whom [you have born] unto me, and these [have you] sac-

rificed unto them to be devoured. Is this [your] whoredoms a small matter.

That [you have] slain my children, and delivered them to cause them to pass though the fire for them?

Ezekiel 23:38–39:

Moreover, this they have done unto me: they have defiled my sanctuary in the same day and have profaned my sabbaths.

For when they had slain their children to their idols, then they came the same day into my sanctuary to profane it; and lo, thus have they done in the midst of my house.

How many women have taken the abortion pill or morning-after pill and then gone into their local church to fellowship?

The recent Supreme Court ruling was a victory for the nation in terms of striking down abortion as a right at the national level. However, this is not a "victory" when some states are now passing the most nefarious, life-denying laws ever in response. Employers are even paying for employees to go across state lines to obtain an abortion if their own state has legislated restrictions due to the Supreme Court decision.

Please ask yourself, *Are we winning this battle?* I assert that we are not because we are fighting it on the wrong front. There have been some amazing, God-sized battle wins.

But most of the troops are on the sidelines. Where are the warriors? Where are the fathers? Women cannot fight this war alone!

Where is the church?

Please pray and ask the Lord to reveal the truth to you about the correlation between abortion and the national demise of our country and ask what you can do about both before it is too late.

Appendix

Meaning of the Names (Author's Version)

Beulah: "married."

Chloe: "spring shoot."

Rachel: "ewe, baby lamb."

Delilah: "delicate."

LeAnn—two words, meaning:

- Le: "clearing in the woods, meadow"
- Ann: (Hebrew origin) "God has favored me," refers to grace

Belinda: "beautiful."

Ling: "spirit, soul, bell, chime."

Ariel: "lion of God."

Willow: "freedom."

Miriam: "wished-for child."

Anayah: "God has answered."

Notes

Biblical references all KJV unless noted.

Dedication

1.   Luke 24:45–48

Preface

1.   1 Corinthians 13:13 (NIV)

Introduction

1.   Acts 20:24

2.   Jeremiah 6:16 (NIV)

Beulah: Clothed in Robes of Righteousness

1.   Isaiah 61:10 (NKJV)

2.   John 6:29, 6:40

3.   Ephesians 2:8–9

4.   Psalm 104:33–34

Perverted Love

1.   1 John 4:7–21 (NIV)

2.   1 John 5:2–3 (NIV)

3.   1 Corinthians 13 (NIV)

Rachel: Blinding Scales and Baby Models

1.   Psalm 103:8–12

My God Is a Star Breather

1.   Psalm 138:2

"And the Dragon Stood on the Shore of the Sea"

1.   Revelation 13:1 (NIV)

Your Dad Has Shot Himself

1.   Psalm 32:7

2.   Psalm 130:1–6

Steady on Love, I'll Make You a Cup of Tea

1.   Psalm 6:8–10

2.   Psalm 116

Ariel: Daughter of Zion

1.   Psalm 86:11–12

2.   Ecclesiastes 7:8

Alice Cooper in Tulsa

1. Psalm 38

2. Jeremiah 23:29

3. Ezekiel 11:19

4. Isaiah 55:11

5. Psalm 40:2–3

You Are Known

1. Psalm 139:1–18

Fallen Trees, Wayward Satellite Dishes, and Gas Leaks—Spiritual Warfare

1. Ephesians 6:10–13

2. Isaiah 41:10

3. Deuteronomy 31:6

Anayah: God Answers Misdirected Call

1. Jeremiah 32:27

2. 1 Corinthians 13 (NIV)

Your Love Is Enough

Appendix

1.   Psalm 104:33–34

A Message in Bottles

1.   Ezekiel 16:20–21

2.   John 1:1–4

3.   Romans 11:15

4.   Isaiah 51:3

5.   Isaiah 61:1–3

6.   Isaiah 62:1

7.   Zechariah 1:14

8.   Isaiah 46:13

Ganei Chaim: Garden of Life

1.   Isaiah 61:11

Bereshit (Genesis): Mathematics of Eternity

1.   John 1:1

2.   Luke 6:40 (NIV)

3.   John 18:37

4.   John 14:6

5.   John 8:12

6. 1 John 5:1–5

7. John 3:16

8. John 8:31–32

9. Revelation 7:9–12

10. Isaiah 62:4 (NIV)

11. Isaiah 62:11–12

Epilogue

1. Ezekiel 16:20–21

2. Ezekiel 23:38–39

Endnotes

1 Hephzibah: "one who evokes delight, one who is guarded, a protected one."
2 Beulah: "married."

CPSIA information can be obtained
at www.ICGtesting.com
Printed in the USA
BVHW061451050723
666787BV00004BB/46